*May the God who is both great and good
make your marriage stronger and your hearts braver.
May He create not only a willingness to die for your
marriage but also a passion to live for it.*

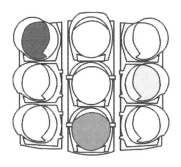

TOGETHER
COMPANION JOURNAL

Reclaiming **Co-Leadership** in Marriage

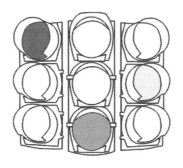

TOGETHER
COMPANION JOURNAL

Reclaiming **Co-Leadership** in Marriage

anne+tim evans

Includes Facilitator's Guide

TOGETHER COMPANION JOURNAL: RECLAIMING CO-LEADERSHIP IN MARRIAGE

Published by REAL LIFE Ministries

PO Box 6800, Colorado Springs, CO 80934

For ordering information visit Amazon.com

All rights reserved. Except for brief excerpts for review purposes, no part of this book may be reproduced or used in any form without written permission from the publisher.

The stories in this book are based on decades of ministry, counseling, and real-life experiences. Names and details regarding some individuals whose stories are told in this book have been changed to protect their privacy. Editorial liberties have been taken to combine certain stories and circumstances for the purpose of clarity and illustration.

All Scripture quotations, unless otherwise noted, are taken from the New American Standard Bible®, Copyright © 1960, 1995 by The Lockman Foundation. Used by permission. (www.Lockman.org.); NIV are taken from the Holy Bible, New International Version®, NIV®. Copyright © 1973, 1984 by Biblica, Inc.TM Used by permission of Zondervan. All rights reserved worldwide. www.zondervan.com; ASV are from the American Standard Version. (Public Domain.) Scripture quotations marked TLB are taken from The Living Bible, © 1971, Tyndale House Publishers, Wheaton, IL 60189. Used by permission.

The authors have added italics to Scripture quotations for emphasis.

© 2014 Tim and Anne Evans

Cover Design: Amy Konyndyk

Printed in the United States of America

First Edition 2014

DEDICATION

We dedicate *Together: Reclaiming Co-Leadership in Marriage Companion Journal* to Dr. Gilbert (and Maria) Bilezikian. As your students, for over three decades we have lovingly referred to you as Dr. Bilezikian, Dr. B, Gil, and our spiritual dad. So many of the co-leadership values and oneness principles we write and teach about go back to what you taught us at Willow Creek Church and in your marriage and family courses at Wheaton College. We treasure your love and friendship beyond words. Your passion for community, oneness, and learning have become lifelong personal and marriage goals. We remain committed to living out, and teaching, the truths, and the life lessons you have given to us, our children, grandchildren, and spiritual children. Gil, we joyfully dedicate this Companion Journal to you and Maria! With much love and respect,

anne+tim evans

"Remember those who led you, who spoke the word of God to you; and considering the result of their conduct, imitate their faith."

Hebrews 13:7

CONTENTS

Introduction: A Note from anne+tim +1

+ PART ONE: GOD'S CO-LEADERSHIP MARRIAGE DESIGN

Lesson 1 – The Traffic Light Principle +9

Lesson 2 – The Starting Place: God's Purpose—the Why of Marriage +17

Lesson 3 – From Good … to Not Good … to Very Good +23

Lesson 4 – Co-Leadership Lost +31

Lesson 5 – Co-Leadership Reclaimed +37

Lesson 6 – Part 1: Did Jesus Say Anything about Marriage? Gender +43
Part 2: Did Jesus Say Anything about Marriage? Sexuality +49

Reflections of the Heart +54

+ PART TWO: PUTTING CO-LEADERSHIP INTO PRACTICE

Lesson 7 – From "Me" to "We" +57

Lesson 8 – Absolutes and Preferences +63

Lesson 9 – Part 1: Equality and Headship +69
Part 2: Submission and Authority +79

Lesson 10 – Love, Respect, and Roles +89

Lesson 11 – Co-Leadership Is Liberating for Everyone   +95

Lesson 12 – Marriage Is Not It   +103

Reflections of the Heart   +109

Further Study   +111

Facilitator's Guide   +117

Additional Challenge   +125

Acknowledgments   +127

About the Authors   +128

REAL LIFE Ministries   +129

INTRODUCTION

A NOTE FROM ANNE+TIM

Change is a difficult thing. Sometimes it's easy to read a book, feel slightly intrigued by or mentally agree with what you read, and then go on with your life without taking steps that will make an impact. This Companion Journal is here to change that—to lead you through challenging questions and help you advance in intimacy with God, your spouse, and others.

As you read our book *Together: Reclaiming Co-Leadership in Marriage*, we want to challenge you to explore these life-giving concepts with your spouse. This Companion Journal is a tool to help you start putting God's original co-leadership marriage principles into practice. You may use the book and Companion Journal as a couple or in a small-group setting. Whatever the case, we're here to walk with you. We've been living out co-leadership principles for thirty-eight years, and we want to cheer on anyone who is willing to take the hard but incredible step of pursuing God's original marriage design.

We know that embracing the concept of being one in marriage is a lifelong journey. Use this journal to meditate on what you've learned, process questions together with the Lord and your spouse, wrestle with new revelations, and take time to prayerfully journal what God is teaching you. Let the truth God brings you soak into your soul and transform your life and marriage.

Lesson Layout

The title of each lesson in the Companion Journal corresponds with the title in *Together: Reclaiming Co-Leadership in Marriage.* We encourage you to read or reread the book as you go through this Companion Journal; it's important to be familiar with the stories and principles found in each book chapter so the material is fresh as you enter the study. We have organized each lesson to help guide you through questions and step into action as you apply what you've learned. We've also provided a user-friendly "Further Study" section in the back of the book that gives every reader opportunities to dig deeper into some natural questions that may come up in the course of this study.

Life Is Lived in a Story

We begin each lesson with a personal story from a married couple who are walking out co-leadership. Their stories illustrate how God has transformed them in the area the lesson covers so you can understand how God wants to transform you and your marriage.

Chapter Overview

This section provides a brief review of the chapter from the book *Together: Reclaiming Co-Leadership in Marriage* that coincides with the lesson in the Companion Journal. While we hope you'll review the chapter itself before starting the lesson, this summary will give you an idea of the direction you'll be taking in each lesson's study.

REAL LIFE Questions

Each lesson includes several questions that invite you to go deeper. Our desire is that the questions will not simply be something you rush through. Go beyond the easy answers we often give in our Christian lives. Our hope is that you will wrestle with the truths the questions are prompting.

REAL LIFE Personal Application

Each lesson includes personal applications that will challenge you to take the truths off the page and apply them to your life and marriage.

REAL LIFE Co-Leadership Application

Here's where it gets fun! The REAL LIFE questions and personal applications lead to this: the chance to partner with your spouse to live out co-leadership *together*. One way to practice is to take turns initiating each lesson's co-leadership challenge.

Don't be afraid to trust and risk as you work through areas in your marriage where you may be experiencing some obstacles. Every journey includes twist and turns in the road—what's important is for you to walk through them *together.* You and your spouse will be growing, advancing in intimacy and oneness as you seek God—and that's where co-leadership becomes powerful.

I.O.T.L. *(Inquire of the Lord)*

Throughout each lesson, we will continue to challenge you to engage with your good Father. Taking time to **I.O.T.L.** *(inquire of the Lord)* is an opportunity to implement step one of the Traffic Light Principle. Invite God into your dialogue and your process by asking Him for wisdom (James 1:5).

Listening to God

Learning how to relate with God is the most important lesson you will ever learn. Growing in listening to Him is a big step toward advancing in intimacy. Recognizing His voice—no matter if it's soft or loud, or whether it comes through His Word, in the form of a new thought, or from a friend—and responding with a willing heart is more important than any book you will ever read or any question you will answer.

As you flip through the pages of this Companion Journal, you will see shaded Listening to God columns. These columns are visual reminders prompting you to actively listen to Him. Becoming a good listener is a learned skill that takes practice. As you process through each lesson, record anything you sense He may be saying in the shaded columns.

Facilitator's Guide

If you are facilitating a small-group community through this study, we have provided a few tips and thoughts to help you along the way. See the last portion of this book for the Facilitator's Guide.

A Few Cautions

+ The **I.O.T.L.** (*inquire of the Lord*) section and the Listening to God columns are just for you—not for the public. If you choose to share with your spouse or someone in your group, that will be your decision. We want this to be a safe place where you can grow in intimacy with God by practicing good listening skills.

- The Lord will never say something or ask you to do anything that does not align with His character. Test what you are sensing and journaling about with Scripture. Remember: God will not contradict the principles in the Bible.
- Don't make any major life decisions simply based on what you sense or think the Lord is saying. For example, decisions about marriage, having children, moving, changing jobs, or making major financial commitments should be shared with a few mature, godly people who can affirm and/or challenge the direction you are sensing.
- Beware of the inner critic—the demeaning voice that minimizes your attempts to advance in intimacy. The Enemy will actively try to restrict you from growing deeper in intimacy with God.

Community

God designed us for community. His very nature reflects and reveals community—God is Father, Son, and Spirit. And for us, His children, there is power in joining together in community and encouraging others as they encourage us. We advance in intimacy when we trust God and risk entering into community with others. So while this Companion Journal can be used individually, we urge you to go through it as a couple or with a small group. God has given us other people for a reason. We see Him reflected and revealed in others, and they can cheer us on and encourage us to walk in our true identity—to be all that God created us to be.

We are excited for you to take this journey. Go forward in hope and joy. Dream and pray for the marriage God designed you to have. Be blessed. We're cheering you on!

anne+tim evans

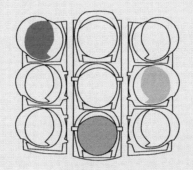

PART ONE

God's Co-Leadership Marriage Design

*Haven't you read ... that at the beginning the Creator "made them male and female," and said, "For this reason a man will leave his father and mother and be united to his wife, and the two will become one flesh"? So they are no longer two, but one flesh. Therefore what God has joined **together**, let no one separate.*

Matthew 19:4–6 NIV

LESSON 1

THE TRAFFIC LIGHT PRINCIPLE

Life Is Lived in a Story

My wife and I had always dreamed of raising our family in Black Forest, Colorado. We were looking for a house and working with a small budget in a big-budget area. It was a time of great uncertainty for us. We had already sold our home and were living with family. Discouragement was setting in as thoughts of plan B were starting to take shape. We were not equipped as a couple to deal with the division we were facing in our marriage over this decision.

During that season, we were invited to attend a REAL LIFE marriage gathering. That was the first time we had heard teaching on the Traffic Light Principle. Being on the same page with God and your spouse was good stuff. As we drove back from the conference, my wife told me she felt complete peace with whatever God had planned next for our family.

The following Tuesday a house became available that was in our desired area and price range—and was large enough to fit our family of six. It sat on five acres of land surrounded by beautiful pine trees. The housing market was competitive at that time, so we had to make a quick decision. We both walked the property and prayed, asking God to direct our steps. Coming back together, we both felt complete peace with God and each other—we both had green lights to move forward. On May 8 we purchased the property of our dreams.

On June 11 our house and thousands of pine trees on our property burned to the ground in Colorado's Black Forest Fire. It was devastating. Through the difficult days that followed, we experienced God's hand of protection on our marriage in amazing ways. We felt His strength, knowing that we had made this decision in unity with Him and each other.

*We began the rebuilding process with a renewed commitment to make every decision by implementing the Traffic Light Principle **together**. The unity that we had with God and each other gave us the strength to work through this stressful time in our lives. We can't imagine what this process would have looked like if we had moved forward without having both included God and each other. The Enemy would have had many opportunities to divide us through blame, shame, and misdirected anger.*

In April 2014 we moved back into our dream home, surrounded by our blackened trees. All we can say is that God is good and the intimacy we have in our marriage is stronger than ever.

+ + +

Chapter Overview

Our closest relationships are often the ones that bring us the most pain. And when you look at the state of marriage today you've got to wonder ... *what are we doing wrong?* Most marriages probably start out the same: with hope, with passion, with love. So how could a relationship designed to bring such joy, a relationship meant to provide us with someone to love deeply and share our lives with, cause so much heartache?

God created marriage to reflect and reveal the most intimate of relationships: the Trinity of God. He created a marriage covenant to be something unique and beautiful. It is more than two individuals becoming one. It is a man and woman inviting God into their sprit, soul, and body oneness. With God as the leader, a Christian marriage is more than 1+1—it is 1+1+1

Unfortunately, we often leave God out of the equation. Husbands and wives try to solve problems without ever turning to the maker of marriage—without ever **I.O.T.L.** (*inquiring of the Lord*), seeking His design and His direction.

Maybe your marriage is at a place where it needs a little life breathed into it—and what marriage couldn't use more life? We want to share with you one practical way God has taught us to strategically invite Him into our marriage.

Meet the Traffic Light Principle.

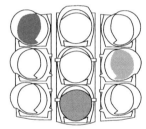

Can you guess who each of the three rows of lights represents? That's right: you, your spouse, and God. Here is our challenge: whenever you and your spouse need to make a decision, implement the Traffic Light Principle.

First, I.O.T.L. (*inquire of the Lord*) individually, then as a couple. After seeking His perspective, come back together, sharing what you sense He is saying. Do you sense Him giving you a green light (go), a yellow light (wait), or a red light (no)? If you're not in agreement, then wait—because *unity* should always *trump disunity*. The key to implementing the Traffic Light Principle is to invite God into your process and

LISTENING TO GOD

wait until you *both* have green lights. Remember, God is much more interested in unity than in either one of you getting your own way.

Then, fasten your seatbelts and get ready for a ride. If you'll let Him, God will use co-leadership to transform every aspect of your marriage.

REAL LIFE Questions

1. We began this Companion Journal with the following prayer:

> *May the God who is both great and good*
> *make your marriage stronger and your hearts braver.*
> *May He create not only a willingness to die for your marriage*
> *but also a passion to live for it.*

List some ways you'd like to see your marriage become stronger and your hearts braver.

_____

_____

_____

List two ways you are willing to die for your marriage.

_____

_____

List two ways you are willing to live passionately for your marriage.

_____

_____

2. As you were growing up, what did you observe about how authority figures in your life (parents, family, friends) made decisions? In other words, how were decisions presented, processed, and resolved?

_____

_____

_____

_____

List the positive things you observed.

_____

_____

_____

List the negative things you observed.

_____

_____

_____

3. Describe a situation in which you and your spouse were faced with an important decision. How was the decision presented, processed, and resolved?

_____

_____

_____

_____

LISTENING TO GOD

4. When you hear the phrase "include God in your decision-making process" or "invite Him into the dialogue," what does that mean personally to you?

_____

_____

5. What steps are you ready to take in order to be more intentional about including God in your Traffic Light decision-making process?

_____

_____

REAL LIFE Personal Application

The Traffic Light Principle is a tool that helps couples make decisions—a tool that begins by including God in your process.

Throughout this study, commit to doing *your part* in the Traffic Light Principle. Invite God into *your* decision-making process, and be open to His direction.

REAL LIFE Co-Leadership Application

Agree to utilize the Traffic Light Principle as a couple. Begin looking at every decision as an opportunity for you and your spouse to invite God into your Traffic Light Principle process. Take note of how including God and your spouse in making decisions increases intimacy and oneness in your marriage.

I.O.T.L. (*Inquire of the Lord*)

Taking time to **I.O.T.L.** *(inquire of the Lord)* is an opportunity to practice implementing step one of the Traffic Light Principle. For example you may want to ask,

Lord, is there anything You want to highlight that was not covered in this lesson? Is there anything You would like me to share with my spouse and/or our community group?

Write down anything you sense.

_____
_____
_____
_____
_____

LISTENING TO GOD

LESSON 2

THE STARTING PLACE: GOD'S PURPOSE— THE *WHY* OF MARRIAGE

Life Is Lived in a Story

My husband is a profoundly kind man and true lover of God and my heart, but I realized that the "gender trump card," though dormant in our marriage and almost never played, still had pinned my heart down in immeasurable ways. When we first heard the message of God's original co-leadership design for marriage, my heart began to burn in my chest. **Really?** *I cried silently.* **Could this be true? You dreamed of co-leadership from the beginning? Oh God! This is amazing!*

Tears streamed down my face. I worshipped God for His kindness, beauty, humility, wisdom, and brilliance—and for the value He places on both men and women. And I was worshipping Him for the rescue of our hearts and marriage.

What fruit this truth has born in our marriage! My husband and I are experiencing a oneness and intimacy we have never known before. While God's growing of our marriage into a co-leadership model has not been without cost, it has caused us to have to really know each other in more intimate and honest ways and come to the center of each other's hopes, dreams, needs, and disappointments. We are freed from the anxiety and dread of making unilateral decisions that don't consider the other person's heart. And we are seeking God's heart in new ways, walking even more in His image as a man and as a woman. Returning to "in the beginning" has helped us experience a unity, partnership, and singleness of heart we never tasted before.

+ + +

Chapter Overview

Have you ever felt lost in your marriage? Have you ever sensed that you and your spouse might have taken a wrong turn, gotten off track along the way, or missed the signs and landmarks that were supposed to lead you to a more fulfilling lifelong marriage partnership?

Feeling lost doesn't have to be an obstacle—it can become an opportunity. You don't have to wander along unmarked trails, wondering what happened in your marriage. What you need is a new perspective, a map that takes you back to the beginning of the trail.

In the beginning ... God created marriage in a world without sin. Think about that for a moment. Marriage as God intended it, marriage in its purest form, is found in only one place in the Bible: before the fall, before sin (Gen. 1-2). Is it possible that after all this time of reading the marriage map for signs of equality, headship, submission, and authority, we've missed the most important signpost of all—the one leading us back to the beginning of the marriage story?

The first marriage relationship was created to reflect and reveal the relationship in the Trinity of God. A man and woman were both created in God's image, a community of oneness that did not include hierarchy, headship, male leadership, or female subordination.

In God's original marriage design, the man and a woman were both invited to **reflect** and **reveal** the plurality of God's nature. They were both commanded to **rule** (exercise dominion) over God's creation, and they were both commanded to **reproduce** more community. In Genesis, the dominion and procreation mandates were given to *both* the man and the woman. God didn't designate any hierarchy when He created marriage. He fashioned a beautiful *mutuality*. So if you're feeling lost in your marriage, perhaps the way to regain your bearing is to go back to the beginning.

REAL LIFE Questions

1. Where you start determines where you end. Where did your marriage start?

_____

_____

_____

2. The marriages you observed growing up often become your map and guide. Take some time to evaluate some of the examples you had for marriage.

What maps were they using? What were some of their obstacles?

_____

_____

_____

_____

3. Describe a specific time when you felt lost on your marriage trail. What did you do to get back on course?

_____

_____

_____

LISTENING TO GOD

What ways were successful?

_____

_____

_____

In what ways would you like a *do-over?*

_____

_____

_____

4. There are a variety of ways couples approach marriage. Briefly describe your current view of marriage. Is it a traditional/hierarchical view? A complementarian view? An egalitarian view? Or God's original co-leadership design that includes mutual equality and mutual authority?

_____

_____

_____

5. Consider this: There is no hierarchy or headship in the Trinity of God. The Father, Spirit, and Son are mutually equal and share mutual authority. Likewise, there was no hierarchy or headship in the first marriage. How does this relate to your perspective of marriage?

_____

_____

_____

In what ways could this impact your marriage relationship?

_____
_____
_____

REAL LIFE Personal Application

Commit to spending time in the Word, read through Genesis 1-2. Ask the Lord to give you His perspective of marriage. Write down what you sense.

_____
_____
_____

Before the fall, the man and woman coexisted in unity and oneness with each other. There was no hierarchy, headship, or female subordination. The Triune God was the head. He was their ultimate authority. Meditate on Genesis 1-2. Review the Further Study section (#2: Hierarchy and the Trinity of God) at the end of *Together: Reclaiming Co-leadership in Marriage*.

REAL LIFE Co-Leadership Application

In addition to using the Traffic Light Principle, agree to give God's original co-leadership mutual equality and mutual authority marriage design a try for the remainder of this study.

> LISTENING TO GOD

Discuss the practical implications of living out co-leadership. How might this change the ways you currently relate to each other?

_____
_____
_____

I.O.T.L. (*Inquire of the Lord*)

Taking time to **I.O.T.L.** *(inquire of the Lord)* is an opportunity to practice implementing step one of the Traffic Light Principle. For example you may want to ask,

Lord, is there anything You want to highlight that was not covered in this lesson? Is there anything You would like me to share with my spouse and/or our community group?

Write down anything you sense.

_____
_____
_____
_____

LESSON 3

FROM *GOOD* ... TO *NOT GOOD* ... TO *VERY GOOD*

Life Is Lived in a Story

*For a long time, my husband and I thought we had problems with his parents. Don't get me wrong: they **were** difficult. But here's what we finally found out: **our problem wasn't actually with his folks**. Our problem was with unity in our marriage.*

My husband is an only child. His parents had always longed for more children. After he and I married, it seemed like his parents tried to use me and our kids to fill that void. My husband and I are both pleasers: He didn't want to disappoint them, and I didn't want to disappoint him. So for years he allowed them to directly and indirectly control us while I allowed resentment to build up. We wrongly blamed our discord on their actions instead of looking to the gaping hole in our unity. You see, if my husband and I had been in unity, issues arising with his parents wouldn't have mattered, because we would have been in agreement about how to handle each situation.

After seeking the Lord and godly counsel, we decided to implement the Traffic Light Principle in every single situation that came up with his parents—to a painstaking degree. We "Traffic Lit" everything from phone calls, to their requests to spend time with our kids, to when and if we would have them over. One time we waited three days to return a phone call because we were not in unity. We applied the Traffic Light Principle to absolutely every decision, no matter how small or basic, because it was the only way we could learn how to function in healthy ways with each other regarding my husband's parents.

It was tedious and hard, but guess what? We are relating to his parents in healthy ways. It took a long time—two years of intentionally undoing the established (negative) reactions in our marriage. However, once my husband and I were in unity over our individual boundaries and our marital boundaries, his parents got used to seeing **us as a we**.

Meanwhile, we have never had more respect for each other about family issues and decisions. I love his parents, and I want them involved with our children—not a sentiment I could have expressed two years ago. I'm so proud of my husband for being willing to apply the Traffic Light Principle to an issue less obvious than finances or a job change, especially because it *was* **his** family, which made the entire ordeal more difficult for him. We are committed to responding to decisions by always first inquiring of the Lord and waiting until we **both** have green lights. We just wish we'd done it sooner. It turned a situation from not good to **very** good.

+ + +

Chapter Overview

"Not good."

That's what God called Adam's aloneness. Adam was in a sinless, perfect world—and yet he was missing out on something very close to God's heart: relationship. So God fashioned someone who would rescue man from his *not good* situation. Think about that: the very first rescue in the Bible involved the woman rescuing the man from his *not good* condition of aloneness.

God created Adam and Eve —*together* —to mirror the essence in community and oneness of the Trinity of God.

We hear the word *helper* or *helpmeet* and often think it means woman was created as an assistant of sorts—but that couldn't be further from the truth. Woman was created to offer her strength, love, and help to the man as a co-leader and equal partner.

Being a *helper* means jumping in when you're needed, acting as a part of a team. It doesn't mean you're greater or less than the one you're helping. Because—as we see in Genesis—God gave the same mandates to both the man and the woman. They were created to pursue God's purposes *together*, naked and unashamed. No fear. No control. No shame or blame. A pure, equal relationship defined by mutual equality (both made in God's image) and mutual authority (both given the pro-creation and dominion mandates).

When husbands and wives recognize that co-leadership is a key to reflecting and revealing the plurality in the Trinity of God, they begin to understand how marriage can become a beautiful expression of who He is. In co-leadership, *marriage is not about me* but includes God and your spouse. This starts with making **I.O.T.L.** *(inquiring of the Lord)* a priority. In other words, God shouldn't just be a part of your relationship—He should be the life and breath of your relationship. Only when we grab hold of that truth and step forward *together* in co-leadership will we see His power explode in our marriages.

LISTENING TO GOD

REAL LIFE Questions

1. Think of a time when you as a couple made a decision *together* in unity. What was the outcome?

_____

_____

_____

Now think of a time when you made a decision and did not have unity. What was the outcome?

_____

_____

_____

2. Review Tim's story about being a *helper*, when as a fire chief he helped a fireman drag a charged line into a building. Describe a situation in which you acted as a *helper* for someone who needed it.

_____

_____

_____

Did you feel a sense of authority because you took that role of helper?

_____

_____

_____

3. Why do you think some people read Genesis's description of a woman being a *helper* and conclude that this indicates she is automatically in a subordinate role under the authority of her husband?

_____

_____

_____

How might this culturally subordinate perspective cause a husband to miss out on all the gifts, blessings, and potential his wife has to bring to the marriage relationship?

_____

_____

_____

4. How might the descriptions of a husband and wife being *one flesh* and *naked and unashamed* help you better understand oneness and co-leadership in your marriage?

_____

_____

_____

5. What are specific ways you could remove any emotional fig leaves of shame, blame, fear, and control and make room for openness, intimacy, and unity?

_____

_____

_____

LISTENING TO GOD

6. Read these words from the chapter: *If marriage is not about me, then who is it about?* How might reorienting your perspective on marriage change how you relate to your spouse and to God?

_____

_____

_____

REAL LIFE Personal Application

Review the marriage mottos in chapter 3:

- + **I.O.T.L**. *(inquire of the Lord)*
- + Unity trumps disunity
- + Marriage is not about me

Write down the one that jumps out most to you and practice it this week.

_____

_____

REAL LIFE Co-Leadership Application

In marriage, couples should look for ways to *help* each other. List a few ways your spouse acts as your *helper*. Affirm your spouse and thank them for loving and serving you.

_____

_____

_____

Now, describe to your spouse some ways you feel they could act as a better *helper* to you.

_____

_____

_____

Instead of following gender roles that are often culturally based, ask your spouse for help in identifying situations in which your unique gifts and passions could *help* you both advance in unity.

_____

_____

_____

I.O.T.L. (*Inquire of the Lord*)

Taking time to **I.O.T.L.** *(inquire of the Lord)* is an opportunity to practice implementing step one of the Traffic Light Principle. For example you may want to ask;

Lord, is there anything You want to highlight that was not covered in this lesson? Is there anything You would like me to share with my spouse and/or our community group?

Write down anything you sense.

_____

_____

_____

LISTENING TO GOD

LESSON 4

CO-LEADERSHIP LOST

Life Is Lived in a Story

We had been married three years and had three young children ages three, two, and one. Life was off to the races. I was working as a worship pastor at a church and had some songs I had written that I was dying to work on as a side project. I didn't think that my wife would see this project as valuable—certainly not in this busy season in our lives.

I had a couple trips planned for work, with three days off in between. My wife decided to take the children to her parents' for the duration of both trips.

*The house hadn't been this quiet in a long time. I decided to call my buddies, move some furniture out of the house, and set up to do a recording called **2 Days in the Same Place**. Video always helps to tell a story, so I announced a house taping to be held the second night of the recording (not to worry—the house would look fine when my wife got home).*

I thought I was doing her a favor by making a project inexpensively, quickly, and during a time we were apart. I didn't understand why she was still bringing it up several years later as such a difficult thing to get over.

Around that time, we were invited to attend a REAL LIFE marriage gathering at a friend's home. That was the first time we heard about the Traffic Light Principle—a simple tool that taught us how to process decisions. It took time to break the habits that we had developed. But we desperately desired unity with God and one other.

As we processed what happened together, I came to the realization that my wife really wanted to be a part of the project. She loved hosting and entertaining in our home. Looking back, and knowing my wife's gifts, I realized that it would have been a much better project if I had included her. The truth is we're stronger when we're **together.** *That's why we are committed to inviting God to lead our marriage as we focus on hearing from Him and waiting for unity.*

+ + +

Chapter Overview

Lies, sin, shame, blame, fear, control. As each of these things crept into the garden of Eden, the beautiful co-leadership God created for marriage became muddled and distorted. The Enemy introduced doubt into the first marriage—doubt of God's goodness, doubt of God's words, doubt of God's marriage design—and that doubt formed a divide between man and woman. Independence and loneliness replaced interdependence and togetherness.

Eve sinned by listening to and believing the serpent's lies about God. She chose independence over interdependence. Adam sinned by passively accepting the Enemy's lies as he failed to engage with the serpent and with his wife.

And after sin, we see co-leadership replaced with male rulership (Genesis 3:16).

Stop and think about that for a moment. Before sin, co-leadership (mutual equality and mutual authority) flourished. Adam and Eve were partners—both created to reflect and reveal God and to rule and reproduce *together*.

Then came sin. Male rulership and female subordination replaced God's original marriage design. Shame, blame, fear, and control entered marriage and caused disunity—as gender hierarchy emerged.

But with God there is always hope. God provided a way for men and women to find victory over sin. This involved a Person—Jesus Christ—becoming the Way.

REAL LIFE Questions

1. Think of a time you allowed shame, blame, fear, and control to creep into your marriage. Describe the circumstances.

_____
_____
_____

How did that impact your relationship?

_____
_____
_____

LISTENING TO GOD

2. Think of a time when you resisted any propensity to shame, blame, or control your spouse. Describe the circumstances.

_____

_____

_____

How did that impact your relationship?

_____

_____

_____

3. Have you observed any tendencies toward male passivity and female independence in your relationship?

_____

_____

_____

List two ways you use to combat these tendencies.

_____

_____

_____

4. Consider marriage before and after sin. What are any predominant patterns you currently see in your own marriage?

_____

_____

_____

REAL LIFE Personal Application

Guilt is related to *behavior*. A person may feel guilty about something they did wrong. Shame is related to *identity*. A person may feel shameful about who they are. Shame is a false identity.

Think about an area where shame has impacted your life. Examine where the Enemy has lied to you. Once you have identified those lies, **I.O.T.L.** *(inquire of the Lord)*—ask God to help you rewrite His truths about your true identity.

> As you process, **I.O.T.L.** *(inquire of the Lord)* to see if you need to forgive yourself, forgive others, or release God from any wrong perceptions you may have of Him.
>
> God has given you victory over sin and shame. What are specific ways you could stop believing lies about your true identity?

REAL LIFE Co-Leadership Application

Identify one way you consistently shame, blame, or try to control your spouse. Write it down, and develop a plan for how you can be more loving and full of grace. If necessary, ask your spouse for forgiveness for shaming, blaming, or controlling them. Explain your plan to your spouse, and ask them to hold you accountable for your responses in the future.

LISTENING TO GOD

I.O.T.L. (*Inquire of the Lord*)

Taking time to **I.O.T.L.** *(inquire of the Lord)* is an opportunity to practice implementing step one of the Traffic Light Principle. For example you may want to ask,

Lord, is there anything You want to highlight that was not covered in this lesson? Is there anything You would like me to share with my spouse and/or our community group?

Write down anything you sense.

_____

_____

_____

LESSON 5

CO-LEADERSHIP REGAINED

Life Is Lived in a Story

A few years ago, my wife began to feel a stirring that I was supposed to move away from my pastoral staff role at our church.

This was a major shift. We had helped start the church several years earlier and were deeply invested there. However, as God began to speak to us separately, we both began to sense that He had something new for us. After an extended time of prayer, fasting, and seeking counsel, we shared our decision with our leadership team. But as we embarked on the journey of figuring out our next step, we discovered we were not in unity on the specifics.

We had been married fifteen years, and we had made most of our major decisions using the Traffic Light Principle. But this time, as we were exploring a door that had opened for us, my wife didn't have a "green light." I, on the other hand, did—and charged ahead like a bull. Due to my own excitement and lack of wisdom, I forgot the principles we lived by. For us, learning to wait on the Lord and each other for unity has been a learning process. Waiting and listening requires maturity and trust in God and each other. It takes practice when we are both being intentional.

After I had pursued the door for several months, it became obvious to both of us that we were out of unity. We both revisited the Traffic Light Principle and made a decision to wait. During that season of waiting, we realized God's blessing on us as we walked together in co-leadership. Since then, we have been learning the blessings and protection of wuiting for unity and the pain of stepping out before we are in unity. We have been learning to trust that our Father speaks in and through our co-leadership. And we are still on the journey ... waiting for Him to bring unity as we commit to listening to God and to each other.

+ + +

Chapter Overview

Your marriage is not about you.

Let that marinate in your heart and mind for a second. Typically husbands and wives dismiss that statement or give it a cursory nod. *Of course it's not about me*, you may think. But we want you to really stop and think about this question: Who is the main character in the story of your marriage?

We're not talking about what you may *want* to do, or what you think you *should* do. We can all resonate with Paul when he says, "For I do not do the good I want to do, but the evil I do not want to do—this I keep on doing" (Rom. 7:19). The important thing is to recognize our struggle and see where we fall short, understanding our desire to control and dismiss our need for God.

Think about a moment of disagreement with your spouse: Do you typically respond in a way that says you truly understand *it's not about you*? That you're part of a Larger Story? And that you are a reflection of the God who created marriage? Or do you live in the smaller story, where self is the main character and your need for comfort and control dictates your actions and feelings?

We challenge you: Recognize it. Acknowledge it. Let God enter in. Only when God is the main character in your story can you live in the strength, power, and protection of covenant as you grow in spirit-soul-body oneness. It's not easy living out co-leadership, because our sin nature wants to drag us away from God's original mutual equality and mutual authority marriage design. But when God is the main character in your story—when you become part of the Larger Story—then you will discover new levels of oneness, unity, and intimacy you've never dreamed possible. And walking together in the unity of co-leadership can impact generations to come.

REAL LIFE Questions

1. How is a *covenant* different from a *contract*?

_____

_____

_____

Life is lived in a story. What story does your marriage tell about living in covenant?

_____

_____

_____

LISTENING TO GOD

2. Share a time when you chose to live in the smaller story (*where you were the main character*). Describe the circumstances and outcome of your choice.

_____

_____

_____

Share a time when you chose to live in the Larger Story (*where God was the main character*). Describe the circumstances and outcome of your choice.

_____

_____

_____

Considering the implications that living in either the Larger Story or the smaller story has on intimacy with God and each other, what steps are you willing to take in order to choose Larger Story living?

_____

_____

_____

3. List two ways God has uniquely gifted you.

_____

_____

List two ways God has uniquely gifted your spouse.

_____

_____

4. Identify two specific ways that you and your spouse could better utilize your individual God-given gifts to bring more intimacy, power, and protection to your marriage.

_____

_____

_____

REAL LIFE Personal Application

Take some time to do a personal inventory. **I.O.T.L.** *(inquire of the Lord)* as you consider this question:

Is it difficult for you to allow someone else to lead, or do you prefer someone else to be the leader? Why do you think that is?

_____

_____

_____

REAL LIFE Co-Leadership Application

Take time *together* with your spouse to talk through the dynamics of your marriage relationship. Discuss the following:

> Do you believe exercising leadership should be based on gender or spiritual gifts? Explain.

_____

_____

LISTENING TO GOD

In what specific ways are you willing to work *together* to cultivate a culture of co-leadership in your marriage?

_____

_____

How might consistently implementing the Traffic Light Principle help you walk out co-leadership in your marriage?

_____

_____

_____

I.O.T.L. (*Inquire of the Lord*)

Taking time to **I.O.T.L.** *(inquire of the Lord)* is an opportunity to practice implementing step one of the Traffic Light Principle. For example you may want to ask,

Lord, is there anything You want to highlight that was not covered in this lesson? Is there anything You would like me to share with my spouse and/or our community group?

Write down anything you sense.

_____

_____

_____

LESSON 6: PART 1

DID JESUS SAY ANYTHING ABOUT MARRIAGE?

A Note to the Reader:

Chapter 6 has been divided in two parts –Part 1 and Part 2 – corresponding to chapter 6 in *Together Reclaiming Co-leadership in Marriage.* Chapter 6: Part 1 will explore gender and Jesus treatment of women. Part 2 will explore sexuality.

Life Is Lived in a Story

When we were first married, we followed traditional gender roles, in part because we were committed to the church, and we were following what the church was teaching.

But later we were privileged to be part of a church that modeled mutual submission and a pre-fall ethic. As we sat under that leadership, many things that had been unclear suddenly came into focus. It had never seemed right to us that God would restrict someone solely based on gender. Nor did we believe that He would give someone gifts and a calling, and then not allow that person to fully operate in them. As we went back and reread Scripture, we began to see how Jesus came to restore God's co-leadership marriage design.

Our marriage relationship matured. We both began to look for ways to encourage each other in our specific gifts and callings. Both of us felt affirmed and fulfilled. There was a new depth in our intimacy that had never existed before.

We continue to be amazed at how strong a relationship built on co-leadership, mutual submission, and mutual authority can be—and how powerful equality and mutuality can be when they are walked out.

+ + +

Chapter Overview

When we explore male-female relationships and gender roles after the fall, we see evidence of patriarchy, misogyny, hierarchy, and forced female subordination. Women abused, forgotten, treated as property. History—and much of how things still are—shows us a world that's off balance when it comes to gender. But, in the fullness of time, God's Son came to earth. Jesus changed everything. He treated women with unheard-of dignity and respect. In regard to marriage, Jesus pointed people back to God's original marriage design (Matt. 19:5-6).

Jesus arrived in a culture that marginalized, dismissed, and abused women—and He treated them as equals. He welcomed women as His followers, showed them honor, and, notably, didn't talk about any post-fall headship, hierarchical, complementarian, or egalitarian marriage views. Religious leaders did not like His approach. Even His disciples were freaked out by it, declaring that if what Jesus was saying about marriage was true, it would be better not to marry (Matt. 19:10).

REAL LIFE Questions

1. Reflect on how Jesus subverted cultural norms regarding the treatment of women during His time on earth. What is your favorite story about how Jesus related to women?

_____

_____

_____

2. Identify some ways women are marginalized today (in marriage, the marketplace, the church, etc.).

_____

_____

_____

How can you better follow Jesus' example of gender equality?

_____

_____

_____

3. When Jesus talked about marriage, He quoted the pre-fall narrative (in Genesis 1-2). What are some ways we might default to the marriage views that are a consequence of the fall (male rulership, traditional/hierarchical, complementarian) when we explore God's original marriage design?

_____

_____

_____

LISTENING TO GOD

REAL LIFE Personal Application

Do you know someone who has been hurt by gender-role perspectives in the church? **I.O.T.L.** *(inquire of the Lord)*. God may invite you to encourage that person. It's God's desire to redeem the confusion around gender misconceptions in the church.

REAL LIFE Co-Leadership Application

Share one example with your spouse of a couple successfully walking out co-leadership. How do co-leadership principles benefit a marriage?

_____

_____

_____

What steps can you take in walking out co-leadership in your marriage?

_____

_____

_____

I.O.T.L. (*Inquire of the Lord*)

Taking time to **I.O.T.L.** *(inquire of the Lord)* is an opportunity to practice implementing step one of the Traffic Light Principle. For example you may want to ask,

Lord, is there anything You want to highlight that was not covered in this lesson? Is there anything You would like me to share with my spouse and/or our community group?

Write down anything you sense.

_____
_____
_____

LISTENING TO GOD

LESSON 6: PART 2

DID JESUS SAY ANYTHING ABOUT MARRIAGE?

Life Is Lived in a Story

Last year we invested in a REAL LIFE marriage gathering on "Intimacy and Sexuality". Being married almost ten years, if we were honest, my husband and I would have described our sexual intimacy as routine. Both of us work, have kids, serve at church, lead a small group, and have very full lives. Frankly, with the pace of our lives, our sexual intimacy had become an afterthought. When we heard Anne and Tim teach about God's co-leadership marriage design, and more specifically that "God is pro sex!" we agreed that we wanted to make some life changes. So we scheduled an intimacy and sexuality intensive with them. Looking back, it was one of the best investments of time and resources we've made in a long time.

We learned that God designed intimacy and sexuality for many purposes—including: celebration, procreation, protection, pleasure, and comfort. We dealt with some sensitive sexual issues—including some negative sexual imprinting from our adolescent and college years—and they helped us develop a sexual agreement that God is using in amazing ways. Our only regret is that we waited so many years to get some help. Recently we purchased **Together Reclaiming Co-leadership in Marriage**—*the co-leadership and Traffic-Light principles they write about are totally transforming our marriage.*

+ + +

Chapter Overview

After looking at Jesus' treatment of women and marriage, this chapter briefly shifts to the last of the four **R**'s discussed in *Together.* In addition to **reflect, reveal,** and **rule,** the final piece of God's design for marriage is **reproduce.** God created marital sex not only as a means to procreate, but also as a means to provide celebration, protection, pleasure, and comfort. God is pro-sex in marriage, but too often couples miss out on the fullness of what He intends for sexual intimacy: a time of oneness and connection as a husband and wife pursue each other's heart, mind, soul, and body.

REAL LIFE Questions

1. Reviewing the four **R**'s for marriage, we have looked at **reflecting, revealing,** and **ruling**. We concluded Part 1 taking a closer look at **reproducing**. Consider God's purposes for marital sex (celebration, procreation, protection, pleasure, comfort).

Which ones are you doing well in?

_____
_____
_____

Are there any you struggle walking out? If so, why?

_____
_____
_____

2. How did you first hear about sex?

_____

_____

_____

How has the information you were given (or lack of information) impacted your view of sex?

_____

_____

_____

How has it impacted your story?

_____

_____

_____

3. In your marriage overall, how do you view your sexual relationship?

_____

_____

_____

How would you say your spouse views your sexual relationship?

_____

_____

_____

LISTENING TO GOD

4. Are there any unhealthy views that negatively impact your sex life?

_____

_____

_____

What steps are you willing to take to advance in your sexual intimacy?

_____

_____

_____

REAL LIFE Personal Application

Review your sexual history and sexual imprinting. Is there anything that triggers shame, blame, fear, or control?

_____

_____

_____

Ask God to forgive you for any sexual sins. Forgive anyone who has sinned against you. Forgive yourself. Release God from any wrong perceptions you have had of Him. If necessary, talk to a pastor or trusted counselor to help you process your sexual past.

REAL LIFE Co-Leadership Application

Talk to your spouse about how you can both create a safe environment to constructively talk to each other about your sexual intimacy. Before you begin, ask God to lead your conversation. Focus on listening to God and to your spouse. Remember, focus on listening to understand rather than to agree or disagree, direct or control, defend, rescue or rationalize. Clarify your understanding by reflecting back what you hear your spouse say. Avoid shaming or blaming. Always extend grace as your spouse shares their story.

Once you have heard from your spouse, review your own story. Take responsibility for anything you've done or failed to do. If necessary, ask your spouse for forgiveness. Forgive yourself.

(Note: We do not encourage sharing specific details of your sexual past with your spouse.)

I.O.T.L. (*Inquire of the Lord*)

Taking time to **I.O.T.L.** *(inquire of the Lord)* is an opportunity to practice implementing step one of the Traffic Light Principle. For example you may want to ask,

Lord, is there anything You want to highlight that was not covered in this lesson? Is there anything You would like me to share with my spouse and/or our community group?

Write down anything you sense.

_____

_____

_____

LISTENING TO GOD

REFLECTIONS OF THE HEART

Pause. Reflect back over these first six lessons and how they have impacted you and your marriage. Take some time to listen to the Lord. Record anything you may be sensing.

_____

_____

_____

_____

_____

_____

_____

_____

One way to honor the Lord when He speaks is to ask:

Lord, is this something You have just for me?
Is it something you want me to hold in my heart?
Or is this something You want me to share with my spouse or others?

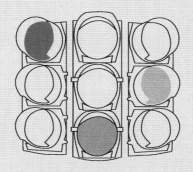

PART 2
Putting Co-Leadership into Practice

There shall be such oneness between you that when one weeps, the other shall taste salt.

Author Unknown

LESSON 7

FROM "ME" TO "WE"

Life Is Lived in a Story

My wife and I attended a REAL LIFE gathering that focused on making decisions together in unity. As newlyweds, we were excited about learning new ways to grow in intimacy with God and each other. We had already experienced several moments of discouragement as we attempted to make decisions as a couple.

Soon after we attend the marriage gathering, we were invited to join a community group with four other couples. Every two weeks we enjoyed a meal with new friends, shared our stories, and talked through each lesson. Being a part of a group allowed us to receive so much wisdom from seasoned couples. It was also a place where we could process what we were learning.

After we implemented the Traffic Light Principle, it was pretty easy for us to come into agreement, but we really struggled with **I.O.T.L.** (inquiring of the Lord). We thought being in agreement was the goal. Therefore, we automatically assumed God was leading whenever we reached agreement with each other.

Our leaders explained that the most important step of the Traffic Light Principle was **I.O.T.L** (inquiring of the Lord). They encouraged us to review the section in Together called "Inquiring of the Lord: Twelve Practical Steps" (pages 112-114).

Implementing these steps helped us confirm what we were sensing from God. This was a game-changer for us! We now bring our decision to God first—and wait until we both have green lights from Him before pulling the trigger. We are so thankful for our community group and the tools we received so early in our marriage.

+ + +

Chapter Overview

Agreement on its own does not create a healthy marriage. A husband and wife can make decisions in agreement and still end up going off-course. The key to a life-giving marriage is including God in your process. He is the One who guides a couple into a dynamic, other-centered, one-flesh relationship.

We've talked about the Traffic Light Principle as a helpful tool in pursuing unity. But it only works when we first **I.O.T.L.** (*inquire of the Lord*)—seeking His direction and asking Him to give a green, yellow, or red light. That's why we've emphasized the importance of listening to God throughout every lesson in this Companion Journal. Following God is not only the most important aspect of a marriage but also the most important aspect of each of our individual lives. Without God leading, we're just wandering in the dark.

I.O.T.L. (*inquiring of the Lord*) goes far beyond a vague sense that we might be hearing from God—because, let's admit it, we can be pretty good about convincing ourselves that what we're hearing is from God when we want something badly enough. **I.O.T.L.** (*inquiring of the Lord*)—seriously inquiring—means being attentive and intentional to verify that what we're hearing is from Him. We pray. We compare what we sense to the Word of God. We ask for the prayers and input of other godly people. We evaluate how what we are sensing will impact the kingdom of God. And we seek to do all of this with a pure heart and from a place of humility and love.

Then, when we sense that what we are hearing is from God—well, that gives us the confidence and courage to follow Him wherever He invites us to go.

REAL LIFE Questions

1. Review the list of the Twelve Practical Steps in chapter 7. Think of a time when you were making a decision. Which of the Twelve steps did you include?

_____

_____

_____

Which steps were not included?

_____

_____

_____

What observations do you make from your choices?

_____

_____

_____

2. Describe one area of your life in which you're *not* asking God for direction?

_____

_____

_____

LISTENING TO GOD

If so, why do you think that is?

_____

_____

_____

How is your decision to include God (or not to include Him) affecting you? Your marriage?

_____

_____

_____

3. Describe one area of your marriage in which you feel you are successfully co-leading in unity with God and with each other? What results are you experiencing?

_____

_____

_____

Describe one area of your marriage in which you don't have unity or are struggling to co-lead together? What results are you experiencing?

_____

_____

_____

How does your relationship with God (individually and as a couple) play into each situation?

_____

_____

REAL LIFE Personal Application

Identify a situation in your life (marriage, family, work, friendships, etc.) in which you made a decision without going to the Lord to ask for His wisdom and direction. Ask the Lord to forgive you. Forgive yourself. Then, **I.O.T.L.** *(inquire of the Lord),* and go through the list of Twelve Practical Steps in chapter 7 of *Together* to make sure you're being intentional about hearing His voice. Write down what you sense He is saying and then act on it. What did He teach you through the situation?

REAL LIFE Co-Leadership Application

Two becoming one in marriage is *not* about a loss of personal identity–it is a process where both partners' identities are enhanced. "You" and "me become "we."

Plan some uninterrupted time for you and your spouse to discuss some practical ways you can advance in becoming "we". Have you been implementing the Traffic Light Principle as a couple since it was introduced in chapter 1?

_____
_____
_____

If so, how do you feel it is working so far in your marriage?

_____
_____

LISTENING TO GOD

If you're struggling to implement it, discuss why do you think that is?

_____
_____
_____

I.O.T.L. *(Inquire of the Lord)*

Taking time to **I.O.T.L.** *(inquire of the Lord)* is an opportunity to practice implementing step one of the Traffic Light Principle. For example you may want to ask,

Lord, is there anything You want to highlight that was not covered in this lesson? Is there anything You would like me to share with my spouse and/or our community group?

Write down anything you sense.

_____
_____
_____

LESSON 8

ABSOLUTES AND PREFERENCES

Life Is Lived in a Story

I was raised in a good home. My parents loved God, each other, and us. My dad was definitely the authority in our home—the one my mom looked to for making the final decision. Don't get me wrong—I remember my parents having plenty of intense discussions around moving, making large purchases, helping us choose colleges, etc. My mom's input was important to my dad, but my dad always had the authority to make the final decision. And that is the model I brought into my marriage.

My wife also grew up in a good home, and her parents also loved God and each other. But their marriage looked a little different from what I was use to. If I had to label it, I would probably call it an egalitarian marriage view. In other words, when decisions were made, the person who was affected the most by the outcome had the final say. For example, when my father-in-law had an opportunity for a promotion that required relocating to another state, he made the final decision. When it was time to pick out the house they would live in, my mother-in-law made the final decision. This marriage view worked for them, or at least it seemed to, from my wife's perspective.

Evaluating how our parents walked out marriage and made decisions didn't seem to matter much when we were dating. In fact, I never remember these being issues until we got married. Let's just say that our first few years were tough. My wife and I are both leaders and have strong personalities, so we had countless late-night discussions that never seemed to get completely resolved. The traditional model I grew up with was my marriage absolute. As a man and a husband, I felt that after listening to my wife, it was my responsibility to evaluate all the data and make the final decision. On the other hand, my wife felt that the egalitarian view that she grew up with was her marriage absolute—that whomever the decision affected the most should have final say in the outcome.

In those early years, we were both unwilling to bend. Over time, our decision-making process seemed to break us down and erode our intimacy. So we decided to extend grace, and surrender our perceived marriage absolutes. But our version of **surrendering and extending grace** didn't work very well. In real life when a decision needed to be made, the strongest person won. And—here's where it really got crazy—when it came time for the next decision to be made, it seemed only fair to let the **other** spouse "win." What started out as grace and surrender ended up looking a lot more like a crapshoot!

We were both confused. Why were the marriage views that worked so well for our parents so divisive in our marriage? Why did our version of **surrender** and **grace** feel more like rolling the dice? It's not that we were resistant to change; we just didn't have any other marriage view to consider.

Then we were invited to a REAL LIFE marriage gathering that focused on decision-making. We heard the co-leadership message for the first time. It was like a light went on in a dark room. Genesis 1–2 suddenly came to light. God's original marriage design looked very different from what either one of us grew up with. We never considered that our individual marriage views could be preferences. We had wasted so many years pridefully holding onto marriage absolutes that divided us. Walking in co-leadership brought a sigh of relief to both of us. Since then, we don't roll the dice. We are committed to living out co-leadership, and we are reaping many benefits in our intimacy and oneness.

Chapter Overview

These days, the world seems to view Christians as absolutists—on everything. It's a generalization, of course, but it seems many Christians are quick to declare that the *Bible says this ... and anyone who believes differently is going against God.*

Of course there are things, as Christians, that we should hold as absolutes. For example, the quintessential oneness of the Trinitarian God (God the Holy Spirit, God the Son, and God the Father); the birth, life, death, and life-giving resurrection of Jesus Christ; the Great Commandment (love); the Great Commission (go); justification by faith; the authority of Scripture; and the priesthood of all believers. These are things that have become the foundations of our faith—our absolutes.

But—and hang with us here—not everything we wrap up in our faith is an absolute. Christianity is full of preferences. For example, some people prefer contemporary worship rather than traditional worship, adult baptism rather than infant baptism, and Calvinism rather than Arminianism. Many passages of the Bible can be interpreted in a number of different ways.

But what about marriage? Some couples *prefer* certain interpretations of debated marriage texts. For ourselves, we *prefer* God's original marriage design; other people *prefer* hierarchical, complementarian, or egalitarian marriage views. We consider marriage views a preference—not an absolute.

REAL LIFE Questions

1. Have you considered the differences between absolutes and preferences in your life? What are the things you hold as absolutes?

___

Do you find consistent support for those things in the Bible?

___

2. What are things you consider preferences?

___

How do you respond to people who believe differently on these issues?

___

3. Think of something you once considered an absolute that you now believe (or are starting to believe) is a preference.

___

What led you to change your perception of that issue?

_____

_____

_____

4. In *Together: Reclaiming Co-Leadership in Marriage*, we suggest the marriage views that emerged after sin entered the story are preferences based on a handful of debated New Testament texts. To get a look at a part of the debate, research some of the different marriage views (you may want to start in the Further Study section of *Together*, but also do a quick online search for "complementarian marriage" and "egalitarian marriage" to see what passages are used to support their views and why). Then, review the pre-fall marriage relationship in Genesis. What strengths and weaknesses do you see in the different marriage preferences?

_____

_____

_____

_____

_____

REAL LIFE Personal Application

Throughout Scripture, we see building up the church and advancing the kingdom of God as top priorities, far above any preferences we might have. List two specific, practical ways you could build up the church and/or advance the kingdom of God through your marriage.

_____

_____

_____

REAL LIFE Co-Leadership Application

Make a date with your spouse to talk about what you are learning. Compare your lists of kingdom-advancing marriage initiatives. Choose one to implement together this month.

I.O.T.L. (*Inquire of the Lord*)

Taking time to **I.O.T.L.** *(inquire of the Lord)* is an opportunity to practice implementing step one of the Traffic Light Principle. For example you may want to ask,

Lord, is there anything You want to highlight that was not covered in this lesson? Is there anything You would like me to share with my spouse and/or our community group?

Write down anything you sense.

_____

_____

_____

LESSON 9: PART 1

EQUALITY, HEADSHIP, SUBMISSION, AND AUTHORITY

A Note to the Reader

Together: Reclaiming Co-leadership in Marriage focuses on God's original co-leadership design for marriage. This marriage view is not taught in most churches or seminaries. We believe understanding the conversations around equality, headship, submission, and authority is foundational to understanding God's original design for marriage. Because we don't want to shortchange this important discussion, chapter 9 has been divided into two parts—Part 1 and Part 2—corresponding to chapter 9 in *Together: Reclaiming Co-leadership in Marriage.* Chapter 9: Part 1 will explore equality and headship. Chapter 9: Part 2 will explore submission and authority.

Life Is Lived in a Story

When we were in our early thirties, our life was full and our marriage was growing. It was exciting to be a part of a dynamic marriage team at our local church. We were privileged to sit under the leadership of seasoned married couples and receive seminary-level training at monthly marriage leadership gatherings.

After being raised in a traditional church, it was refreshing to be part of a church that valued and empowered women by affording them the same opportunities as men. Women were regularly encouraged to use **all** the gifts God had given them. Church leaders didn't just talk about letting women lead; they celebrated women and their gifts, and they eagerly opened doors for women to serve in every church leadership role and function. This included women elders, board directors, teachers, preachers, and ministry leaders.

After one of our marriage team gatherings, our leader asked us if we would be willing to travel to a nearby church and share our hearts for God and marriage, talk to their church leaders about our marriage team training, and facilitate a question-and-answer time. After praying about his request, my wife and I both had green lights.

The other church was a traditional denomination that had existed for centuries; they met and worshipped in a sanctuary that we were told was over one hundred years old.

Our first impression with this church's leaders was quite memorable. When the pastor approached us, he did not acknowledge or make any eye contact with my wife. Instead, he looked me directly in the eyes and asked, "Will your wife be teaching any sessions tonight?" I replied that we would be team-teaching, and I asked him if that would be a problem. He declared rather firmly, "If your wife is teaching any sessions by herself, I and other church leaders will have to excuse ourselves from her teaching sessions."

At first, we thought he was kidding, but then I realized he was completely serious. I thought to myself, **But my wife is the one to whom God has given an amazing teaching gift.** And as he turned and walked away, it dawned on me that this pastor had not made any attempt to greet or acknowledge my wife—who was standing right beside me the entire time.

When we returned to our church marriage leadership team, we shared our story. One seasoned elder smiled and said, "You have just experienced the gender bias that is operating in many churches, seminaries, and denominations."

We asked him to explain what he meant. He replied, "Most churches have a leadership/authority structure in place that has been birthed out of ancient, male-dominated, hierarchical, patriarchal soil.

Practically, this involves women not being treated functionally as equals with men."

Since that encounter many years ago, we continue to share God's pre-fall—mutual equality and mutual authority—marriage and gender views. And sadly, we continue to experience pushback from male rulership, hierarchical, traditional, and complementarian marriage/gender proponents.

All that is to say, as we look back over decades of living out God's original co-leadership marriage design of mutual equality and mutual authority, we regularly thank God for surrounding us with elders, pastors, mentors, and spiritual parents who were passionate about God's original co-leadership marriage design and who courageously supported gender equality.

+ + +

Chapter Overview

Equality and headship. These buzzwords have been the source of endless debate in the church.

In male rulership and traditional-hierarchical-complementarian marriage views, equality is clarified—yes, husbands and wives are *intrinsically* equal, but not *functionally* equal. Husbands are the leaders. Wives are told to focus on complimenting and submitting to their husbands.

LISTENING TO GOD

Similarly, most religious leaders believe that *headship* means the husband has functional authority and—unless something is immoral or illegal—the right to have the final say in making decisions. Figuratively speaking, the husband possesses a gender trump card. Essentially there is a functional hierarchy: the husband is first, and the wife is second. A main passage used to support this is Ephesians 5: the man is seen as the "head" of the wife as Christ is the "head" of the church— and the husband has the final say.

From our study of Scripture, we believe that the "Christ as head of the church" metaphor has been misinterpreted, misunderstood, and misapplied. As we shared in *Together: Reclaiming Co-Leadership in Marriage,*

> As we look to Jesus as our model for headship, do we see Jesus ever having the final say in making decisions? Does Jesus ever pull out a trump card or impose His will or make people comply? For example, does Jesus ever impose His desire for a person to avoid sin, repent, pray, serve at church, tithe, or live in certain ways? (p. 130)

We believe that before sin entered the world (Gen. 3), there was no designated hierarchy, headship, or female subordination. In Eden the man was never declared the leader or spiritual cover. Headship is never mentioned until thousands of years after God's original marriage design. In the beginning the husband and wife enjoyed mutual equality—intrinsically and functionally.

Nevertheless, if headship is a major focus for traditional husband and wives, we encourage the husband to live out headship as the Ephesians passage describes. The husband is to love his wife "as Christ also loved the church" (Eph. 5:25). As head, Christ died for the church; likewise, biblical headship includes a husband denying himself, dying to selfishness, and placing his spouse's needs and feelings above his own. Headship lived out in those ways is utterly Scriptural.

In addition, most male rulership and traditional-hierarchical-complementarian marriage proponents believe that as part of his headship role the husband is also the wife's spiritual cover. Practically, this means a wife goes through her husband for guidance and spiritual direction, and she defers to him in decision making because, as head, he is the spiritual leader in marriage.

Scripture says: "For there is one God and one mediator between God and [human] kind, the man Christ Jesus." (1 Timothy 2:5 NIV). We believe that men and women—husbands and wives—are to go directly to Jesus Christ; they are not to first go through any person—spouse, saint, or religious leader.

If headship and the husband being the leader and wife's spiritual cover are foundational components in the marriage relationship, wouldn't Jesus have laid these things out as absolutes when He discussed marriage? But instead, Jesus talked about the one-flesh principles of Eden (Matt. 19:4–6). He never mentioned headship or the husband being the leader.

In the beginning, God created marriage to be a reflection of the essence of the Trinity of God. Men and woman were created to co-exist in unity and equality–both intrinsically *and* functionally.

LISTENING TO GOD

REAL LIFE Questions

Equality

1. Define equality.

___

What is the difference between intrinsic and functional equality?

___

How is equality lived out in your marriage?

___

2. Read the following passage: "So in Christ Jesus you are *all* children of God through faith, for *all* of you who were baptized into Christ have clothed yourselves with Christ. There is neither Jew nor Gentile, neither slave nor free, nor is there male and female, for you are *all* one in Christ Jesus" (Gal. 3:26-28 NIV).

How does this passage relate to gender equality?

___

Headship

3. Define headship.

_____

_____

_____

Review Genesis 1-2. Do you find any mention or evidence of headship? The man being the designated leader? The man being the wife's spiritual cover?

_____

_____

_____

4. Review Ephesians 5. Do you believe that the husband has the final say in making decisions—a male gender trump card, if you will?

_____

_____

_____

Does Jesus, as Head of the church, ever use a figurative headship trump card?

_____

_____

_____

LISTENING TO GOD

Who has the final say in your marriage? Why?

_____

_____

_____

5. Do you believe that the husband is the wife's leader and spiritual cover?

_____

_____

_____

If so, how do you support that position biblically?

_____

_____

_____

REAL LIFE Personal Application

Chapter 8 of *Together Reclaiming Co-Leadership in Marriage* provided some interpretations of Scripture commonly used to support different marriage views. In the last lesson, you studied a general overview of these passages, but now choose one on the topic of equality or headship and dig deeper into it. **I.O.T.L.** *(inquire of the Lord),* read commentaries, and research different viewpoints to broaden your perspective on what that particular controversial passage might mean regarding headship or equality.

REAL LIFE Co-Leadership Application

Together, talk to your pastor or a trusted spiritual mentor about their perspectives on equality and headship. By hearing from others, you become more aware of how gender is viewed in your church or by those you trust. If invited, share your perspectives and what you have been learning about co-leadership in marriage through this study.

I.O.T.L. (*Inquire of the Lord*)

Taking time to **I.O.T.L.** *(inquire of the Lord)* is an opportunity to practice implementing step one of the Traffic Light Principle. For example you may want to ask,

Lord, is there anything You want to highlight that was not covered in this lesson? Is there anything You would like me to share with my spouse and/or our community group?

Write down anything you sense.

_____

_____

_____

LISTENING TO GOD

LESSON 9: PART 2

EQUALITY, HEADSHIP, SUBMISSION, AND AUTHORITY

Life Is Lived in a Story

"I won't marry you until you're more teachable and submissive."

If you want to talk about words that crush a girl's soul, those get pretty close.

It was bad enough that they came from the man I'd wanted to marry since I was fifteen. It was worse knowing they ultimately came from our pastor, his longtime mentor.

The church I'd grown up in was a place of quiet grace, but it had changed with the hiring of a new pastor. Women were marginalized and dismissed from the pulpit. My parents left the church when the pastor preached that wives were sinning if they ever dared confront their husbands about sin. "Wives, zip your lip and shut your mouth" were the exact words. Angry, dark words that made me feel anxious, but I was going to marry the church golden boy, so I couldn't really leave, now could I?

And then came the soul-crushing words. Our pastor had affirmed my boyfriend's fears about me—my liberal arts education was turning me into an unsuitable wife, and I needed to be called to account.

I ended the relationship, but I blamed church leader's teaching about submission for screwing up my life. And I walked away from God. I spread bitter, biting anger with a collected group of bitter, biting *friends. I sobbed when a visiting female Bible professor talked about the value of women. I didn't want to follow a God who had created one gender to be less-than. Who gave men the authority to determine what I could and could not do–basically telling me I wasn't good enough.*

I didn't realize my church had created a false God.

And then the real God showed up.

I was working for a Christian publisher, of all things. Faithless, rebellious, not going to church, and working on Christian books. And God gave me my story in someone else's words. He sat down next to me as I curled up in the middle of my floor, held me in His arms, and whispered, "I love you, My sweet daughter." Rebellion and bitterness and all.

When the real God stepped in, everything my church said and did suddenly seemed very small and unimportant. My fight about submission faded into confusion. "Why does the church get You so wrong?" I asked Him. He smiled, quietly pushed me down a few new paths, and led me through the doors of another church.

Where the topic the first Sunday was submission.

Well, crap*, I thought.*

And then the pastor got up, opened his Bible, and said, "This is the word of the Lord: 'Submit to one another out of reverence for Christ.'"

He talked about the beauty of men and women serving each other as equals. About how marriage isn't this mess of men being right and women saying yes. How God created us to be so much more together.

I was a messy, weeping puddle in my seat. I felt waves of healing in that room. After years of feeling dismissed and censured by a pastor and a church for my struggles with the idea of submission, God was using another pastor and another church to affirm who He created me to be. He was starting to show me the beauty of mutuality and unity.

LISTENING TO GOD

+ + +

Chapter Overview

Here are two more buzzwords that continue to fuel debate in the church: submission and authority.

Let's start with submission. The *s-word* often comes with lots of negative baggage. In Ephesians 5, Paul introduced a revolutionary New Testament concept that focused on *mutual* submission. Ephesians 5:21 says, "Be subject to one another in the fear of Christ." This other-centered command was not only for husbands and wives but for *all* followers of Christ. In Ephesians 5:22 (NASB) Paul goes on to say, "Wives, *be subject* to your own husbands, as to the Lord." Traditional-hierarchical-complementarian marriage proponents often connect submission to authority. Yet nowhere in this passage is a wife commanded to submit to the *authority* of her husband.

Many Christian couples base their marriage theology on Ephesians 5. The apostle Paul understood authority and hierarchy; if he wanted, he could have clearly designated a hierarchy where the man had authority over his wife. In fact, in the first verse of the next chapter Paul commanded, "Children, obey your parents" (Eph. 6:1). Likewise, Paul could have easily commanded, "Wives, obey your husbands," but he didn't. Instead he introduced to a male-rulership culture a brand-new marriage view of mutual submission (Eph. 5:21). This was unheard of in a culture that didn't value women.

At the end of Ephesians 5, the apostle Paul went back to the beginning. He returned to God's original marriage principles and quoted Genesis 2:24: "For this cause a man shall leave his father and mother, and shall cleave to his wife; and the two shall become one flesh."

Now let's take a look at the word *authority*. We believe authority is at the heart of much marriage misunderstanding and debate. Most interpretations and discussions surrounding headship and submission relate to authority. Over the years, traditional-hierarchical-complementarian marriage-view proponents have described authority in different ways. Some husbands say that as the leader they have a 51 percent role in making decisions and the wife has 49 percent. But *how is a 51/49 functional authority any different from a husband who has 99 percent authority and a wife who has 1 percent?* Either way, the husband has final authority to make decisions.

Other husbands describe their authority as being *the first among equals*. What does *first among equals* mean? It seems that if a husband is *first*, his wife is *second*. The words *first* and *second* denote a hierarchy. Other husbands say (somewhat tongue in cheek), "As the leader, I have authority to make all the *major* decisions in my marriage, but after decades of marriage, we've never had one *major* decision." This statement seems to indicate that the husband is abdicating responsibility in his perceived authority role, and that he does not recognize his wife as having mutual authority.

The only time *authority* between a husband and wife is specifically mentioned is in 1 Corinthians 7:4: "The wife does not have *authority* over her own body, but the husband does; and likewise also the husband does not have *authority* over his own body, but the wife does." The Bible clearly commands *mutual authority* to both the husband and wife.

God's overall theme for life and marriage is mutual submission (Eph. 5:21) and reciprocal servanthood (Phil. 2:3-4). The reality is that it's possible to submit without love, but it's impossible to love without submitting. Bottom line, after all is said and done, *love* is the ball game.

REAL LIFE Questions

Submission

1. Review Ephesians 5:21. If you have a study Bible or concordance, also look through the many *one another* statements found in Scripture. What general principles might you draw about marriage based on these *one another* commands?

_____

_____

_____

How does Ephesians 5:21—"be subject to one another in the fear of Christ"—fit into those principles?

_____

_____

_____

LISTENING TO GOD

2. The original translation of Ephesians 5:22 in the New American Standard Bible reads, "Wives, to their husbands, as to the Lord." Bible translators later added the phrase "be subject" to this text. Why do you think Bible translators added this phrase?

_____

_____

_____

Authority

3. Those who try to establish a hierarchical authority structure of man over woman often use 1 Corinthians 11:3 to support their position. Review what theologian Dr. Gilbert Bilezikian said about this (see page 136 in *Together: Reclaiming Co-Leadership in Marriage*). How do you interpret this passage?

_____

_____

_____

4. Review 1 Corinthians 7:4: "The wife does not have *authority* over her own body, but the husband does; and likewise also the husband does not have *authority* over his own body, but the wife does." How does the *mutual authority* in this passage impact a husband and wife?

_____

_____

_____

How does this passage align with marriage proponents who believe the husband has authority over his wife?

_____

_____

_____

5. Review the story in chapter 9 where Marvin describes himself as the pilot and his wife as his copilot. How does his illustration compare with God being the pilot and each couple being His copilot? Which way do you prefer?

_____

_____

_____

REAL LIFE Personal Application

Spend some time alone with the Lord as you ask Him to help you take an honest look at some areas in your life.

Does the *s-word* carry any negative baggage for you?

_____

_____

_____

Is it difficult for you to submit to your spouse?

_____

_____

_____

LISTENING TO GOD

Women: Do you ever feel a tendency to abdicate authority to your husband? If so, why do you think you do that?

_____
_____
_____

Men: Have you ever felt the need to have the final say? Or have you ever wanted to check out because of the weight of your perceived leadership role? If so, what are ways that you could respond differently?

_____
_____
_____

REAL LIFE Co-Leadership Application

Share with your spouse what you are learning about submission and authority. If you feel comfortable, discuss with your spouse what you discovered about yourself in the REAL LIFE Personal Application section.

In what ways would walking out mutual submission and mutual authority as co-leaders advance your intimacy with God and with your spouse?

_____
_____
_____

I.O.T.L. (*Inquire of the Lord*)

Taking time to **I.O.T.L.** *(inquire of the Lord)* is an opportunity to practice implementing step one of the Traffic Light Principle. For example you may want to ask,

Lord, is there anything You want to highlight that was not covered in this lesson? Is there anything You would like me to share with my spouse and/or our community group?

Write down anything you sense.

_____

_____

_____

LISTENING TO GOD

LESSON 10

LOVE, RESPECT, AND ROLES

Life Is Lived in a Story

Love, respect, and roles have helped us navigate tough spots in our marriage, but they have also become a stumbling block when not properly understood and applied. We have seen how my giving respect to my husband has brought life and encouragement to him. We have experienced how my husband loving me well has brought greater confidence and joy into our relationship. However, like so many things in our walk with the Lord, it becomes easy to turn good things into rules. We take the spirit of what God wants for us and make it a law that we need to follow.

My husband could feel he was loving me well by leading our family and taking charge. I could feel I was respecting him by submitting to his leadership and going along with what he thought was best. It sounds like it should work pretty smoothly.

However, our experience has been that while I can "respect" and "go along" with his decision, I often end up feeling discounted, not loved, and not respected. Ironically, my husband often ends up feeling unloved and disrespected even when I agree to let him lead because my respect really isn't respect at all, and the feelings I bury while trying to respect him end up surfacing in some other area of our relationship. We have reached the conclusion that each of us needs more than just respect or just love—we need both.

*I remember a time when my husband had an opportunity for a lateral job change. It was the kind of decision that affected him more than me. It wouldn't require a move or even a change in company. But it would be a significant change. He came home, and we chatted about it. I could have easily deferred to him in what he wanted to do. He knew the job and understood the changes that would take place in his day-to-day routine. In reality, I didn't have a lot of insight into the situation because of my limited understanding of who reported to whom and what was required of the different roles. But that's not to say that I didn't have anything to offer in the process. We prayed and inquired of the Lord, believing that He loves us and has good plans for us—***together**.*

*We had a few days to process, and we weren't really feeling a clear answer. One of my gifts is discernment, and as I continued to pray about it, I felt like the Lord gave me a picture to share with my husband. After I shared it with him, we both felt like he should take a risk and make the change. Looking back, I'm not convinced that staying in his original position would have been bad. The change he made didn't include a huge raise or promotion. Choirs of angels didn't start singing as he started his new position. But it was a great moment for us in our marriage. It meant a lot to me that he valued my input, even when the decision affected him more than me. He respected the way I heard from the Lord, and he respected my discernment. He knew that I was praying and interceding on his behalf because I love and respect him. After being married over ten years, we have found that we **both** need to give and receive love and respect.*

Chapter Overview

We all need love, and we all need respect. The danger in the conclusion that men need respect and women need love is that it deemphasizes life-giving love and respect needs that both men and women have. A wife may go out of her way to respect her husband, but does it really matter if she isn't showing him love? And we believe it's impossible for a husband to truly love his wife without striving to show her respect.

It's the same with roles. Too often in Christianity we place people in gender specific categories—"you are a man, so you're a leader"; "you are a woman, so you are made to submit and follow"—rather than seeing men and women as intrinsically and functionally equal and encouraging them to maximize all of their God-given gifts. The church and marriages miss out on so much when women are empowered to use their gifts only in predetermined ways.

Every man and woman is made in the image of God, and we all exhibit unique aspects of God, regardless of gender. As you walk out your marriage, set aside any functional inequality and hierarchy, and choose to love and respect each other well as you follow Jesus—*together*.

What about roles in marriage? Remember what we talked about in *Together: Reclaiming Co-Leadership in Marriage*:

> We believe the primary role for every man and woman is to live out the Great Commandment—love. In marriage, we encourage both husbands and wives to focus on the role of being a servant. They are to humbly walk together as co-leaders and reciprocal servants and function in the gifts God has given each of them, doing what works best in their marriage; of course this is different for different couples. Together they celebrate unity and diversity, rather than trying to force each other into predetermined roles based on gender. (p. 155)

LISTENING TO GOD

REAL LIFE Questions

1. Do you believe that love and respect are gender exclusive?

_____
_____
_____

2. As you observe the life of Jesus Christ, do you think He focused more on love or respect?

_____
_____
_____

3. How do love and respect play out in your marriage?

_____
_____
_____

4. Give some examples of the ways you and your spouse function based on gifts rather than on predetermined roles that are based on gender.

_____
_____
_____

5. Jesus described Himself only one time in the Bible. Matthew 11:29 says, "I am *gentle and humble in heart.*" Are *gentleness* and *humility* words you would use to describe yourself? Your spouse?

_____

_____

_____

REAL LIFE Personal Application

In this chapter Tim describes his desire to be known as a man who loved God with all his heart, soul, mind, and strength; a one-woman man who passionately loved his bride well for a lifetime; a man who captured the hearts of his wife, kids, spiritual kids, grandkids—a man who was a faithful spouse, a great dad and granddad.

Write down how you would like to be known.

_____

_____

_____

REAL LIFE Co-Leadership Application

Plan a date together where you can spend time enjoying each other. Talk about how love and respect plays out in your marriage. Ask your spouse what makes them feel loved and what makes them feel respected. Commit to intentionally do those things. Ask your spouse to share with you when they feel a lack of love or a lack of respect.

LISTENING TO GOD

I.O.T.L. (*Inquire of the Lord*)

Taking time to **I.O.T.L.** *(inquire of the Lord)* is an opportunity to practice implementing step one of the Traffic Light Principle. For example you may want to ask,

Lord, is there anything You want to highlight that was not covered in this lesson? Is there anything You would like me to share with my spouse and/or our community group?

Write down anything you sense.

_____
_____
_____

LESSON 11

CO-LEADERSHIP IS LIBERATING FOR EVERYONE

Life Is Lived in a Story

It was the year we celebrated our tenth wedding anniversary. A few months before the actual anniversary, the phone rang. It was my husband's parents, asking him to put them on speaker so I could be a part of the conversation. They started by saying, "We have a surprise for you both—we want to take you on an all-expense-paid anniversary vacation. We've arranged everything, including child care!"

Let me give you a little backdrop to this story. We had been talking about planning something special for our anniversary. We both wanted to go on vacation for a long time, but something always seemed to get in the way. We were either having a baby, or moving, or unable to get the time off work, or the kids got sick, or we didn't have the money. So you can only imagine my initial reaction to an all-expense-paid vacation offer.

To top it off, everything seemed to line up. We were both able to take time off work, we were comfortable with the child-care arrangement, the vacation spot they picked out was amazing, and we really needed a vacation. To me this was a no-brainer.

However, a few years earlier, we began investing in REAL LIFE marriage gatherings. As we were growing in our understanding of intimacy with God and each other, we agreed to live out co-leadership in our marriage. We also committed to implement the Traffic Light Principle.

Initially we both responded to their invitation with enthusiasm that sounded a lot like, **Let's buy the tickets and lock in the plans!** *As the conversation ended, we thanked them for their generous gift. My husband said we'd pray about it and get back to them.*

I remember thinking, **Isn't an all-expense-paid vacation a slam-dunk kind of prayer?** *What kind of God would give us a red light for an offer like this? I had an immediate bright green light—and I was sure the Lord did too.*

We spent the rest of the night talking about how much we needed a vacation and how much fun it would be to get away. We went to bed that night agreeing to pray and give it twenty-four hours. The next evening we put the kids to bed and sat down to talk. I told my husband about my bright green light and was expecting to hear the same from him. But he explained that he spent the afternoon **I.O.T.L** *(inquiring of the Lord)—and while he was fully expecting a* **green** *light, in his heart he sensed a* **red** *light.*

That was not the response I was expecting. I had already mentally packed my bags and was heading for a quiet beach. In a mild panic, I told my husband, "Let's keep praying and see if we don't both get green lights." He agreed.

Over the next few days, as we both continued to pray and process, I kept thinking something would change, but it didn't. After a few days, he was still "red" and I was still "green." That's disunity. As disappointed as I was, we agreed that my husband would call and try to explain to his parents why we were not taking them up on their generous offer.

You can only imagine his parents' response when they heard we were not going—especially after our enthusiastic response just a few nights earlier. They asked lots of questions. Thankfully, my husband did his best trying to explain the unexplainable to his parents. His mom and dad love the Lord, and they love us. They reluctantly accepted our decision, but we both knew they were confused and disappointed.

Our ten-year anniversary was still coming up. We prayed, reviewed our budget, and decided to load up our pop-up camper and reserve a campsite. My husbands' parents graciously offered to provide childcare. As we drove to the campground, a part of me was still dreaming about the vacation offer we had turned down. But our week camping ended up being much more than I imagined. We had perfect weather and a private campsite. We had unlimited time to talk, hike, and ride our bikes. I didn't realize how badly we needed this time alone together to play—to dream—to reconnect.

When you think about it, giving up an all-expense-paid vacation in exchange for a week in a pop-up camper makes absolutely no sense. I thought I knew what we needed, but God knew the deeper needs in our hearts and marriage. As we drove home, we thanked Him for directing our anniversary plans.

We've been using the Traffic Light Principle for years, but we still feel like we're "practicing." We don't always get it right—sometimes one of us runs ahead and comes to a conclusion without inviting God or the other person into the process. But we are so committed to unity that we are quick to apologize and gently remind each other that God is our pilot—we're following Him, not our own desires. God's design for unity is liberating even when it doesn't make sense.

+ + +

LISTENING TO GOD

Chapter Overview

Co-leadership is walked out when both partners submit to God and to each other. It's a beautiful thing. A husband and wife are each free and supported by the other to live out their true identity in Christ. God is glorified, and the kingdom advances. The Traffic Light Principle is such a great marriage tool. The key is to **I.O.T.L.** (*inquire of the Lord*) and wait for both the husband and wife to have green lights.

Are you up for a challenge—for a change? Change involves risk, and transformative change is never easy. But God is raising up a generation that is hungry for something *more* than many marriages they have seen that lack passion and purpose. God is breathing hope and life into couples and inviting them back into the marriage relationship that He crafted *in the beginning*.

REAL LIFE Questions

1. Co-leadership encourages interdependence instead of independence (or unhealthy co-dependency). Think about two specific examples in which you have co-led with your spouse. What was the outcome? List both positive and negative aspects of co-leadership in action.

_____

_____

_____

2. In chapter 11 of *Together Reclaiming Co-Leadership for Marriage*, we describe three hypotheses:

Hypotheses 1: One of the consequences of the fall was given to the woman in Genesis 3:16. "To the woman God said: 'Your desire will be for your husband, and he shall rule over you' " Consider wives who have an inordinate desire for their husbands to take the role of leader, be their spiritual cover, and have the final say in the decision-making process. *Is it possible these wives are living out a marriage view rooted in the consequences of the fall rather than in God's original co-leadership marriage design?*

Hypotheses 2: In the beginning God gave *both* the husband and the wife the procreation mandate and rulership (dominion) mandate. Consider couples who prefer a marriage view that includes the husband having a primary leadership role and functional authority. *Is it possible these wives might be abdicating their God-given authority as co-leaders together with their husband?*

Hypotheses 3- Consider husbands who have an inordinate desire for possessing authority, being the leader and spiritual cover, and having the final say. *Is it possible these husbands are living out a marriage view rooted in the consequences of the fall, after which God said to the woman, "And he shall rule over you?" (Gen. 3:16b)*

3. Identificational repentance means to stand in or represent the offender—to identify with their sin and apologize on their behalf to those who have been offended. In Chapter 11 of *Together: Reclaiming Co-Leadership in Marriage*, Tim says he wants to ask women for forgiveness on behalf of those who have offended them: "As a man, husband, ordained minister, and male church leader, on behalf of myself and countless men, husbands, ministers, and male church leaders who have been unkind, unfair, and discounting ... *I am so sorry.*" How do you feel about this apology?

LISTENING TO GOD

_____

_____

_____

What are some of the ways you see marriages and churches missing out because women are restricted from using all of the gifts the Holy Spirit has given them?

_____

_____

_____

REAL LIFE Personal Application

Change involves risk and getting messy.

As you consider walking out God's original co-leadership marriage design, what parts involve risk? What parts are messy?

_____

_____

_____

REAL LIFE Co-Leadership Application

Plan time alone with your spouse. As you continue to process God's original co-leadership marriage perspective, consider the power of repentance. Romans 2:4 says, "...the kindness of God leads you to repentance". Is there anything you need to ask your spouse forgiveness for? (Both sins of commission—what you did—as well as sins of omission—what you failed to do.)

_____

I.O.T.L. (*Inquire of the Lord*)

Taking time to **I.O.T.L.** *(inquire of the Lord)* is an opportunity to practice implementing step one of the Traffic Light Principle. For example you may want to ask,

Lord, is there anything You want to highlight that was not covered in this lesson? Is there anything You would like me to share with my spouse and/or our community group?

Write down anything you sense.

_____

_____

_____

LISTENING TO GOD

LESSON 12

MARRIAGE IS NOT IT

Life Is Lived in a Story

We both grew up in traditional church homes. For us, believing in God was about following His rules rather than being in relationship with Him. During our first year of marriage, we were invited to a church that was meeting in a movie theater in the northwest suburbs of Chicago. It was called Willow Creek Community church.

The simple message of the gospel literally changed the course of our lives.

Seeking first the kingdom of God was something we learned **together**—as a couple. God used our marriage as a vehicle to teach us about His plurality and goodness. As we grew closer to God, individually and **together**, He used our marriage to advance His kingdom. When we loved and forgave each other, we understood His love and forgiveness toward us on a deeper level. When we surrendered or extended undeserved grace to each other, we understood the love and grace our good Father extended toward us on a deeper level.

Everything we experienced in marriage was a lesson about living in the kingdom of God. Seeking first the kingdom of God was something that flowed out of us—through our marriage—and into the world. We were invited to reflect and reveal the oneness found in the triune unity and community of God.

We were invited to co-lead (to rule) **together**, *and we were encouraged to reproduce (biological and spiritual children).*

Advancing the kingdom of God was not so much about what we were doing, or the ministry we were involved in, or the gospel presentation we were making. The kingdom of God is me—it's you—it's "we." It's marriage—it's love birthed in the heart of a triune God.

+ + +

Chapter Overview

We hope that after this study, you understand the importance of seeking first the kingdom of God. To advance His work. To glorify Him—*together*.

God created something extraordinary when He created marriage. But marriage is not the end goal—marriage is not "it." Glorifying God is the primary goal in the life of a fully devoted follower of God. And you can glorify Him in amazing ways through your marriage.

We began both this Companion Journal and our book with the following prayer:

> *May the God who is both great and good*
> *make your marriage stronger and your hearts braver.*
> *May He create not only a willingness to die for your marriage*
> *but also a passion to live for it.*

Review how you answered the following questions in lesson 1. Would you answer them any differently now? (Page 12)

_____
_____
_____

List some ways you'd like to see your marriage become stronger and your hearts braver.

_____
_____
_____

List two ways you are willing to die for your marriage.

_____
_____
_____

List two ways you are willing to live passionately for your marriage.

_____
_____
_____

LISTENING TO GOD

What if ...

What if God's original co-leadership design for marriage was reclaimed? How would that impact you? Your church? Your community? Your city?

_____

_____

_____

REAL LIFE Questions

1. What are two dreams you have for your marriage?

_____

_____

_____

2. Review the epilogue in *Together: Reclaiming Co-Leadership in Marriage* about our second attempt to climb Pikes Peak. What "cairns" have you followed in your marriage journey?

_____

_____

_____

What marriage "cairns" do you want to erect for others to follow?

_____

_____

_____

3. What changes have you seen in your marriage as you've explored co-leadership principles throughout this study?

_____

_____

_____

REAL LIFE Personal Application

Identify areas in which you struggle to live out co-leadership. Ask for God's help, and write down a strategy for overcoming those struggles.

_____

_____

_____

REAL LIFE Co-Leadership Application

Plan a date. Go out to dinner, go for a hike—whatever allows you time to relax and enjoy each other's company. Find creative ways to celebrate the work you've done in your marriage. Dream *together* about what God could do in the coming days. What would you like the next chapter in your story to say?

_____

_____

_____

LISTENING TO GOD

I.O.T.L. (*Inquire of the Lord*)

Taking time to **I.O.T.L.** *(inquire of the Lord)* is an opportunity to practice implementing step one of the Traffic Light Principle. For example you may want to ask,

Lord, is there anything You want to highlight that was not covered in this lesson? Is there anything You would like me to share with my spouse and/or our community group?

Write down anything you sense.

_____

_____

_____

REFLECTIONS OF THE HEART

Pause. Reflect back over lessons 7–12 and how they have impacted you and your marriage. Take some time to listen to the Lord. Record anything you may be sensing from Him at this time.

_____

_____

_____

_____

_____

_____

_____

_____

One way to honor the Lord when He speaks is to ask:

Lord, is this something You have just for me?
Is it something you want me to hold in my heart?
Or is this something You want me to share with my spouse or others?

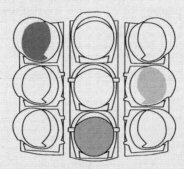

FURTHER STUDY

A Note to the Reader:

In the Further Study Section on page 201 at the end of *Together: Reclaiming Co-Leadership in Marriage*, you'll find several short topical discussions that help you dig deeper into some of the concepts discussed. These questions can be answered individually, as a couple, or in your small group.

The following questions align with each of those fourteen topics:

1. **Equality and Mutuality:** How does understanding the equality and mutuality found in God's original marriage design affect how you view your relationship with your spouse?

_____

_____

_____

Is there anything you need to change to reflect marriage "in the beginning"?

_____

_____

_____

2. **Hierarchy in the Trinity of God:** Have you been exposed to the concept of hierarchy within the Trinity of God? After reading this section, how do you feel about that opinion?

_____

_____

_____

What do you believe about subordination in the Trinity and ontological equality?

_____

_____

_____

3. **Different Genesis Accounts:** What have you typically believed about the nature of the Genesis accounts? Are they allegorical? Literal?

_____

_____

_____

How do your views impact your understanding of the principles of God's original marriage design?

_____

_____

_____

4. **Gender Equality:** Review Philip Payne's twenty points regarding the equality of men and women in the pre-fall account. Which points struck you most deeply, and why?

_____

_____

_____

5. **Man Naming the Woman:** Have you ever heard this contextual discussion of the naming of the man and woman in the Genesis account? What does it say to you that "God *formed* man"(Gen. 2:7) and "God *fashioned* woman" (Gen. 2:22)?

_____

_____

_____

6. **God Speaking to the Man First:** What are the implications, if any, of God speaking to the man first?

_____

_____

_____

Do you believe that this is a sign of authority?

_____

_____

_____

LISTENING TO GOD

If so, how is it different from Jesus speaking to Mary first after He rose from the dead?

_____
_____
_____

7. **Returning to Eden:** What are the differences between literal and figurative language in the Bible?

_____
_____
_____

List some examples of figurative language, either from Scripture or from our culture.

_____
_____
_____

8. **Treatment of Women:** Do some research on Jesus' treatment of women and how women were treated in the early church. How does this inform your thoughts about the place of women in the body of Christ?

_____
_____
_____

9. **Theology:** How does your theology relate to your faith? The Bible says, "Knowledge puffs up while love builds up" (1 Cor. 8:1 NIV). Have you ever sensed yourself leaning too much on your knowledge and not enough on love?

_____
_____

What steps can you take to help you grow in love?

_____

_____

_____

10. **Biblical Method of Interpretation:** Have you studied Scripture in the way described?

_____

_____

_____

Go to one of your favorite Scripture passages and apply these principles to it. What new perspectives do you gain about the passage?

_____

_____

_____

11. **Authority:** Review the revolutionary ways that Paul honored women. How does this better inform your understanding of his statements regarding marriage?

_____

_____

_____

LISTENING TO GOD

12. **Jesus—the Quintessential Servant Leader:** What are your thoughts on this statement about Jesus as the quintessential servant leader?

___

What are some ways you can act as a better servant leader in your marriage?

___

13. **Slavery:** Do you see any similarities between the commentary on slavery and the current debate about gender roles? How might understanding that cultural context help you better dialogue with those you disagree with about co-leadership and gender equality?

___

14. **Protestant Reformation:** Do you believe God still speaks? Do you believe He steps into our stories and provides greater illumination regarding how He wants us to live? If so, how might this be similar to God providing greater illumination in regard to returning to His original co-leadership marriage design?

___

FACILITATOR'S GUIDE

Sometimes the most powerful journeys happen in community. We have seen God work in incredible ways in our time studying God's original co-leadership design for marriage with different couples. As you will see in many of the stories shared throughout this Companion Journal, when God enters in and walks *together* with a couple, amazing things happen. Gifts are unleashed, unity is strengthened, and often marriages are saved.

While this study is one that can be completed alone with your spouse, we encourage you to seek the "iron sharpens iron" experience of studying in community. To that end, we have provided this facilitator's guide.

Facilitators guide the group's time together and provide structure so everyone may benefit from a focused, intentional study. Remember that each group is different—feel freedom within the basic structure we've provided in this guide. This Companion Journal contains twelve lessons. In addition, Lesson Six and Lesson Nine are divided into two parts. We have also included a Further Study lesson.

Together process what will work best for the group in regard to scheduling your gatherings.

Given the nature of this study, and our belief that husbands and wives bring different valuable perspectives and gifts to the table, we suggest that a husband and wife facilitate the study *together* as partners. Depending on the maturity of the group, you may want to have different couples facilitate specific lessons.

Materials Needed

Each person should have a Bible, a copy of this Companion Journal, and every couple should have a copy of *Together: Reclaiming Co-Leadership in Marriage*. It is vital for couples to interact with the material in the book as well as in the Companion Journal. As the facilitator, bring extra pens and paper for those people who may want to take notes but forgot to bring note-taking supplies.

Preparing for the First Gathering

We want to offer a few suggestions as you prepare to facilitate a Together community group:

- Begin with prayer—**I.O.T.L** (*inquire of the Lord*). Agree with your spouse to invite God into each step of your process. Ask God to help you choose the members in your community group. Make sure you and your spouse both have green lights on each person.

- Facilitators create an atmosphere where couples can interact, connect, and grow. Once your group has been selected, schedule a time for everyone to meet before the study begins. You may want to share a meal, and have everyone bring a dish. As you make introductions, ask each person why they want to be a part of this study. Take turns telling your stories. Set the stage as facilitators by going first. The level of vulnerability and transparency you model directly impacts the intimacy level of your group.

A Few Important Notes

- Our prayer is your community becomes a team. Communicate to your team the importance of being available and teachable. Have each team member agree to make attendance a high priority, read the correlating chapter in the book, complete each section of the Companion Journal lesson, be prepared to participate in the discussion, and come ready to receive from the Lord.

+ Trust and confidentiality are vital to any healthy team. Commit as a group to honor one another by not letting anything said in the group leave the group. This study walks through potentially difficult subjects. Give one another the gift of freedom to be vulnerable and transparent throughout the course of this study.

+ Honor every person in the group. Don't let anyone dominate the discussion. Recognize the different personalities while creating a safe place for introverted group members to share.

Lesson Structure

+ Depending on the group size, we suggest allowing two to three hours for every lesson. Make sure you commit to start and end on time—you want to respect the schedules of the other people in the group. Set some time aside for socializing at the beginning, but gauge how much time you think you'll need for study and discussion, and make that the priority.

+ Begin each meeting with prayer—**I.O.T.L** (*inquire of the Lord*). This is so foundational to advancing in intimacy with God, your spouse, and members in your group.

+ Quickly review the chapter overview and, if needed, the chapter in *Together: Reclaiming Co-Leadership in Marriage*.

- Walk through each question in the Companion Journal for that lesson. If a particular question does not lend itself to group discussion, either skip over it or restructure it to better fit the group.

- Guide the discussion gently, and be aware if discussion of a particular question becomes too time consuming or gets off-topic. While you can linger on a question if it's proving to be particularly important or helpful to the group, you'll also want to allow enough time to cover the entire lesson.

- The REAL LIFE Questions, Personal Application section, **I.O.T.L.** (*inquire of the Lord*) section, and Listening to God columns are to be worked through individually. The Co-Leadership Application section is designed for couples to work through together. Remind group members they have permission to share as much as they feel comfortable with.

- Close with prayer. Ask couples what encouragement they might need, either from the week's lesson topic or in their marriage in general. Commit to pray for one another throughout the week. You may want to suggest that the men in the group take turns pairing up with other men as prayer partners, and the women with the women.

- Exchange contact information (telephone numbers, email addresses, home address, etc.)

Lesson Guidance

Each lesson is laid out in a manner that allows facilitators to guide the discussion. We have provided additional guidance that highlights suggested areas to focus on.

Throughout the study, continue to encourage the group to utilize the **I.O.T.L.** (*inquire of the Lord*) section as well as the Listening to God columns. Practicing two-way communication (talking and listening) is key to advancing in intimacy with God and others.

Lesson 1

Begin the discussion by asking the group about their initial reactions to the Traffic Light Principle. If there is any confusion about the principle, revisit the longer explanation of it in *Together: Reclaiming Co-Leadership in Marriage*. At the end of the lesson, ask if any of them are willing to take the REAL LIFE Co-Leadership Application challenge and implement the Traffic Light Principle. Doing so should not be a requirement of this study, so make sure you emphasize the freedom to simply come and learn. If any group members state their willingness to try the Traffic Light Principle, however, commit to regularly asking one another about how it is going over the course of the study.

Lesson 2

Some group members may be feeling some pain after this week's lesson if they are facing particular obstacles in their marriage and feeling a sense of hopelessness. Begin your time by reading 1 Corinthians 7:28, "Those who marry will face many troubles in this life" (NIV). Share either a current or past marriage obstacle in which you and your spouse felt hopeless. Cultivate an atmosphere of vulnerability and safety, and encourage group members that any sense of being "stuck" or "lost" in their marriage doesn't have to be their long-term reality. Ask group members if anyone is planning on living out co-leadership over the next three months. Again, doing so should not be a requirement of this study, so make sure you emphasize the freedom to simply come and learn.

Lesson 3

This lesson covers some of the nitty-gritty issues we face regarding the Genesis account. Start your time together by asking group members about their current perspectives on the marriage relationship in the Genesis account.

Lesson 4

Review the shame, blame, fear, and control destructive patterns that emerged after the fall. Ask group members for their reactions toward anne+tim's suggestion that marriage before the fall (God's original design) and marriage after the fall were very different things.

Lesson 5

Ask group members if they've ever looked at their lives in the context of living in the Larger Story versus the smaller story. Explore together how group members feel about the practical implications of God being the main character in their story.

Lesson 6: Part 1 - Gender

Ask for group reactions to the idea that Jesus changed the paradigm of how women were viewed and treated in the ancient world. Ask women in the group how they feel about gender views in the church. Ask men to respond to the women's comments on church gender views.

Lesson 6: Part 2 - Sexuality

Be sensitive to where couples are at in their sexual intimacy. Talk to the group about maintaining healthy boundaries when sharing stories. If deeper issues surface, encourage individuals/couples to seek Christian/pastoral counsel.

Lesson 7

You are halfway through the Companion Journal. You may want to plan a social community group outing—a chance for couples to continue to connect outside of the study group.

Review the "we" marriage concept. Ask couples to share how this plays into co-leadership.

Lesson 8

Begin the lesson by asking people to share their absolutes. Then ask them to identify things Christians may consider to be absolutes that could be described as preferences. Make sure this discussion is honoring; if necessary, remind group members that the purpose of this discussion is not to criticize other people's perspectives, but to acknowledge that parts of our faith involve more shades of grey than many often think about.

Lesson 9: Part 1 and Part 2

Before beginning this discussion, acknowledge the difficulty and controversy surrounding equality, headship, submission, and authority. Ask group members to commit to honor one another in what they say and how they say it. If the discussion gets too heated, remind group members of this commitment.

Lesson 10

Encourage group members to share a time when their spouse showed them love or respect, regardless of stereotypical gender perspectives. Ask them to share about their spouse's giftings. Let this be a time of celebrating one another.

Lesson 11

Ask group members to share about any recent co-leadership victories they may have had. Discuss whether they have found co-leadership liberating, or whether they are still struggling to implement it. Use this time to allow group members to encourage one another in their marriages.

Lesson 12

Ask group members about how focusing on co-leadership and **I.O.T.L.** (*inquiring of the Lord*) has helped them begin to understand the bigger-picture view of how God wants to use their marriage. At the end of your time together, challenge group members to pursue the dreams they've shared and to live in the Larger Story.

Further Study

Feel free to cover one or two of these questions each week of the study, or as the group members raise questions about these topics on their own. If you have a separate meeting time to cover all these questions, combine it with a time of celebration and fun. You and your group have completed a life-changing marriage study—celebrate what God has done!

ADDITIONAL CHALLENGE

Thank you for investing in our *Together: Reclaiming Co-Leadership in Marriage Companion Journal*. We encourage those interested in marriage and gender issues to invest in further study. First **I.O.T.L.** (*inquire of the Lord*), and invite the Holy Spirit to guide you. John 16:13 says, "When the Holy Spirit, who is truth, comes, he shall guide you into all truth" (TLB). We suggest you begin with the Bible: start in Genesis 1:1—"In the beginning." Ask God to help you envision what His original design for marriage was like *before* sin entered the marriage story. Compare the mutual equality and mutual authority—co-leadership—in God's original marriage design to later-spawned marriage views that included hierarchy, male authority, and female subordination.

Regarding later marriage views, countless sermons have been preached, and numerous books and blogs have been written about equality, headship, submission, and authority. In *Together* we prayerfully chose to invest only one chapter on these topics. Instead, our primary focus was on God's original marriage design. Nevertheless, for those wanting to explore perspectives that align with traditional marriage views, we offer the following resources:

+ A website that provides scholarly information, free articles, book reviews, and a blog from traditional-hierarchical-complementarian gender and marriage perspectives is the Council for Biblical Manhood and Womenhood (CBMW) at http://cbmw.org/.

+ Two websites that provide scholarly information, free articles, book reviews, and blogs from an egalitarian perspective are Christians for Biblical Equality (CBE) at http://www.cbeinternational.org/ and The Junia Project at http://juniaproject.com/

For an excellent egalitarian presentation about gender, read "A Challenge for Proponents of Female Subordination to Prove Their Case from the Bible" by Dr. Gilbert Bilezikian. His full challenge can be found at http://www.cbeinternational.org/?q=content/challenge-proponents-female-submission-prove-their-case-bible.

ACKNOWLEDGMENTS

+ Life is lived in a story, and writing this book has been a story of God bringing a team—*together*. A few key REAL LIFE team members include: our Prayer Shield Team; our family, children, grandchildren, and spiritual children; and our spiritual parents and mentors.

+ Thank you to special REAL LIFE friends and partners: Jim and Kathy Kubik, Keith and Robyn Brodie, TJ and Deb Bratt, John and Therese Tekautz, Steve and Pam DeBoer, Linda and Tim Laird, George and Melodee Cook, Danny and Angela Gieck, John and Meredith Blase, Jared and Megan Anderson, Paul and Barb Osburn, Justin and Valerie Ensor, and many others.

+ Thank you to Caitlyn Carlson—your passion for living out co-leadership in marriage and your creative manuscript input and professional editing have been priceless. To Amy Konyndyk—working with you on our REAL LIFE branding, cover design, and interior layout has been so life giving.

+ A special thank-you to the couples who wrote the real-life stories for each chapter—thank you for sharing a part of your lives and story. And thank you to the men and women in our marriage and community small groups throughout the decades—seeing you advance in intimacy with God, and watching you co-leading *together*, inspires us to stay on the trail.

+ We thank God for and we bless others who will build on what we have written about gender equality and co-leadership in marriage. We believe God still speaks. The Bible reminds us, "We know in part," (1 Cor. 13:9), and we sense that God is getting ready to provide fresh revelation about togetherness in mutual equality and mutual authority—what we call co-leadership. Our prayer is that God builds a co-leadership marriage team, a network of relationships united in heart about a mission—God and marriage—that matters.

+ Lastly, we thank God for creating marriage, intimacy, and sexuality. Father, it's our prayer that Your original together-ness in co-leadership marriage design is passionately reclaimed and humbly restored.

ABOUT THE AUTHORS

anne+tim evans are a real-life couple who love marriage. For thirty-eight years they have passionately explored the miracle and mystery of two becoming one in the context of God's original co-leadership marriage design. They are parents, grandparents, pastoral counselors, and spiritual parents. Tim is a retired fire chief; Anne is a licensed nurse and certified Life Purpose Coach. They are both ordained ministers, have master and doctor of practical ministry diplomas from Wagner Leadership Institute, and are nationally certified Healing House Network ministers. They enjoy their marriage, kids, and grandkids; friendships; hiking; motorcycling; and living in Colorado near Pikes Peak. *Together* they lead REAL LIFE Ministries full time.

REAL LIFE MINISTRIES

+ REAL LIFE Ministry's mission is to help men, women, and couples advance in loving God, loving a spouse, and loving others (Matt. 22:37–40) through:

+ Pastoral counseling
+ Pre-marital counseling
+ Marriage tune-ups
+ Marriage intensives
+ Marriage Advance Seminars
+ Forgiveness workshop
+ Communication workshop
+ Overcoming Destructive Cycles workshop
+ Intimacy and Sexuality workshop
+ Restoring the Foundations: www.restoringyourlife.org
+ Life coaching and life plans (anne): www.lifepurposecoachingcenters.com
+ Men's and Women's Advances

tim+anne evans

REAL LIFE Ministries
www.RLmarriage.com
PO Box 6800
Colorado Springs, CO 80934

To purchase *Together: Reclaiming Co-leadership in Marriage* books/ebooks, or *Together: Reclaiming Co-leadership in Marriage Companion Journal,* visit www.amazon.com.

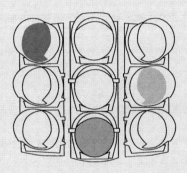

Haven't you read ... that at the beginning the Creator "made them male and female," and said, "For this reason a man will leave his father and mother and be united to his wife, and the two will become one flesh"? So they are no longer two, but one flesh. Therefore what God has joined *together,* let no one separate.

Matthew 19:4–6 NIV

Made in the USA
Middletown, DE
11 September 2015